THE RACE WHISPERER

The Race Whisperer

Barack Obama and the Political Uses of Race

Melanye T. Price

NEW YORK UNIVERSITY PRESS

New York

NEW YORK UNIVERSITY PRESS
New York
www.nyupress.org

References to Internet websites (URLs) were accurate at the time of writing. Neither the author nor New York University Press is responsible for URLs that may have expired or changed since the manuscript was prepared.

Library of Congress Cataloging-in-Publication Data
Names: Price, Melanye T., author.
Title: The Race Whisperer : Barack Obama and the Political Uses of Race /
Melanye T. Price.
Description: New York : New York University Press, 2016. |
Includes bibliographical references and index.
Identifiers: LCCN 2016010269 | ISBN 9781479853717 (cl : alk. paper) |
ISBN 9781479819256 (pb : alk. paper)
Subjects: LCSH: Obama, Barack—Oratory. | Rhetoric—Political aspects—
United States—History—21st century. | United States—Race relations—
Political aspects—History—21st century. | Communication in politics—United States—
History—21st century. | United States—Politics and government—2009-
Classification: LCC E908.3 .P75 2016 | DDC 973.932092—dc23
LC record available at http://lccn.loc.gov/2016010269

New York University Press books are printed on acid-free paper, and their binding materials are chosen for strength and durability. We strive to use environmentally responsible suppliers and materials to the greatest extent possible in publishing our books.

Manufactured in the United States of America

10 9 8 7 6 5 4 3 2 1

Also available as an ebook

For the Spates, Price, and Gordon women!

I am because you are!

CONTENTS

ACKNOWLEDGMENTS

The argument and case studies for this book came to me pretty easily and fairly early into the Obama presidency. It took much longer to write. My ideas come in quick sprints, but manuscripts require a marathon of intellectual, physical, and spiritual effort. I am tremendously grateful for the people who ran this marathon with me. It is important to me that I name those people who will get no credit (and after reading this book may not want any) but have helped me shape this book in important ways.

This book is my second collaboration with NYU Press and Ilene Kalish. She is always open about the process, responds quickly, ensures a timely turnaround, and is encouraging. Without a publisher, there is no book. Without an editor who sees the value in your book, there is no publisher. I am so thankful that for the second time, she has seen the merit of my work. I am also thankful to Kate Babbitt whose editing improved this book greatly.

In 2010, I joined the Rutgers faculty, and I have never received better mentoring and professional advice. I was welcomed into a strong and diverse intellectual community. This embrace began in my home department of Africana Studies. I am so thankful for this scholarly community, which includes Edward Ramsamy, Kavitha Ramsamy, Gayle Tate, Kim Butler, Walton Johnson, Karla Jackson Brewer, and so many others. My office neighbor, Denniston Bonadie, gets a special shout out for his willingness to read drafts and talk through ideas. Coming to Africana Studies also meant that I would engage with the best support staff in the world. These women have helped me in so many ways, and I would not be as happy at Rutgers without their presence. Veronica Reed and Summiya Abdul-Quddus, thank you for your kindness, encouragement, and laughter. I am also a member of the Political Science Department, where I have thoroughly enjoyed my interactions with colleagues. In particular, Lisa Miller and Cyndi Daniels read this manuscript and offered helpful comments. Additionally, Sue Carrol, Kira Sanbonmatsu, Beth Leach, Andy Murphy, and Sophia Jordan Wallace have been great colleagues. At Rutgers, I gained and lost one of the best colleagues ever, Alvin Tillery. Navigating those first few years would have been impossible without his help.

Beyond my departments, I have had the opportunity to interact with one amazing and generous scholar after another. When you study race, you often find yourself as the only person—or one of the few—doing what you do on your campus. The bench at Rutgers is so deep I haven't even met everybody. My first two years were happily spent as a member of the Narratives of Power Workshop in the Rutgers Center for Historical Analysis. The workshop, led by Deborah Gray White and Donna Murch, introduced me to wonderful colleagues and helped me hone this project. Randal Maurice Jelks stepped in to read several chapters at the last minute and provided valuable comments and encouragement.

On a whim and because of a desire to explicitly integrate more feminist analysis into my work, I audited Mary Hawkesworth's Feminist Knowledge Production seminar. It was the best rash decision I've made in a long time. The readings from that seminar directly resulted in a published article, a partial book chapter, and a visit to the Poconos. From our first meeting, Mary was kind and generous with her time and expertise. Shatema Threadcraft and Brittney Cooper are crucial to my success at Rutgers, and their impact on my life has been enormous. These women are funny, smart, productive, and a joy to be around, and in their presence, I get to be all those things too. Everybody needs a Tema and Brit in their lives, but these two are all mine.

I have been fortunate enough to carry friends from one stage in my life to the next. They remind me of who I was and who I want to be. The beauty of Facebook is that we are able to keep up with and encourage each other from afar. For this project in particular I want to thank Salina Gray, who remains a model for what it means to live by the principles we developed as young kids at Prairie View A & M. Watching her move through life reminds me of the things I wanted to accomplish back then and to integrate Prairie View Melanye into the woman I have become now. In my last book, it was pointed out to me that I thanked a bunch of people but left one name out by mistake. Big ups to Carlton Watson! I've lived quite a few places since undergrad and he is one of the few people who has shown up to every city and looked me up. That's friendship. From my grad school crew, I am happy to still have the support and friendship of Valeria Sinclair-Chapman, Kathy Powers, Javonne Paul, Khalilah Brown-Dean, Cynthia Duncan Joseph, and Raquel Greene who have opened their homes to me, shared rooms with me at conferences, and so much more. I am lucky to have colleagues whom I have the privilege to also call friends. Wendy Smooth and Byron D'Andra Orey have had the pleasure of listening to arguments about this book for years and never got tired of hashing things out with me. Though I was happy to leave my professional life in Connecticut behind, I was sad to leave a great community. Kerry Kincy, Renee Johnson Thornton, and Katja Kolcio and their families are dearly missed. For twenty years, I have had an amazing best friend, Gloria Hampton, who knows all my secrets and still wants to be friends with me. I am grateful for her friendship and for her addition of Kara and Marcus Peterson to my life.

Unexpectedly, my life in New Jersey rekindled some relationships and established indispensable new ones. For the first time in two decades, I live in the same city as one of my relatives. My cousin Michelle Spates reminds me daily how easy it is to love her and bonds me with the memory of my beloved Uncle James. In many ways I have become closer to both of them again and it has been a tremendous gift. Somehow in the transition to New Jersey I became friends with Michael Benn again and his support during the writing of this book was a wonderful surprise and invaluable in the grueling final days of completing the first draft. For the first time in over a decade, I also found a spiritual community whose love and prayers cover me. It all started out as a way to get a little bit of church and lot of brunch with Pastor Leslie Callahan and Rev. Charisse Tucker. Somehow, I am a member of St. Paul's Baptist Church and a trustee. This congregation has truly embraced me and my heart is warmed by my interactions with them. The Callahans (Leslie and Bella) and Tuckers (Charisse, Dianne, Hardrict, and Tyree) have been instrumental in this journey back to religious life. I have also developed wonderfully supportive relationships with Lisa and Dana Miller, Theresa Jones, and many others.

If you talk to me more than five minutes, I will mention my family. They are my safe harbor, my North Star, my home. I dedicated this book to the women in my family, but I am lucky to also have a host of nieces, nephews, great-nieces, great-nephews, and cousins who keep me grounded and showered in love and laughter. I have a lot of sisters, and they take being a good sister seriously. In their presence I am the baby sister again and I feel like I can take on the world. Thank you so much Sandy, Leslie, Sharon, Melynda, and Shawana. In many ways and in different ways, they make a better person. I especially thank Melynda for James Efrain Price. He is an awesome little gift! My Aunt Mary has been my cheerleader since birth. If I need a prayer or a pep talk, hers is the first name that comes to mind. She is also the mother of three cousins who are as close to me as sisters—Kathryn,

Erica, and Wanda. I am lucky to be in a family that models sister-hood in the best and healthiest ways. While my Uncle Joe was living with my mom, we talked nearly every day. He had great confidence in my ability and a ready laugh for all my jokes. We talked about this book and President Obama incessantly, and he was very excited and encouraging about this project. I am sorry that he won't be here to celebrate it. There is no person that I am more indebted to in my life than Sandra Faye Spates Price! I have benefited from her sacrifice and hard work tremendously. She is my walking, talking hero and I cherish her! For all that I have and do, I thank you most of all. How cool it is that you have two daughters with books coming out in the same year!! You rock!!

Last, while writing this book, I lost Jewel Limar Prestage, a pre-cious mentor and champion. Her presence in my life changed its tra-jectory forever. I have no doubt that there would be no grad school, no doctorate, no dissertation, no articles or books without her nudg-ing (and sometimes shoving) me toward this life. So grateful to be one of Jewel's jewels; it's really rarified company.

There are many people to thank and I am sure that I have missed some important names. Charge it to my head and not my heart. And of course, any faults in this book are all mine! I happily take credit for this project and I am super proud of it.

Introduction

race whisperer (n): one who is seamlessly and agilely able to employ racial language and tropes by using personal experiences or common historical themes to engage and mobilize diverse racial constituencies.

President Obama's remarks on July 19, 2013, took everyone by surprise. Nearly a week after George Zimmerman was found not guilty of killing Trayvon Martin, an unarmed African American teen on his way home from a convenience store in Sanford, Florida, who Zimmerman had pursued after being told by an emergency dispatcher to remain in his car, President Obama walked into the White House Press Room and began to speak from handwritten notes about the ordeal (Landler and Shear 2013). News channels interrupted regular programming, correspondents working in the White House went from slowly making their way into the room for yet another briefing to sprinting at the sound of the president's voice, and Facebook and Twitter lit up with the news that the president was giving live comments about Trayvon Martin. For the first time since the beginning of his presidency and five years after his historic election in 2008, Barack Obama stood in front of the American people and spoke plainly and honestly about race, a case that had held the attention of American people for the previous two years, and a trial that was the center of a summer media blitz.

The president began with a slightly reluctant cadence to explain why he had gone off script and schedule on this particular day. After instructing the reporters that he would not be taking any questions, he began the substantive part of his address by mentioning his previously released written statement regarding the verdict, reiterating that he would not rehash the details of the actual trial, and extending his prayers to the Martin family. Then he shocked most observers by taking on the popular refrain that "Trayvon Martin could have been . . . me 35 years ago." Indeed, Black men of all ages strongly identified with a kid walking home with snacks he had purchased during a break from watching the NBA All-Star game. This was also very much a reiteration of President Obama's previous statements that "had his wife given birth to sons instead of daughters, they would look like Trayvon Martin" (Thompson and Wilson 2012). He then went on to talk personally and poignantly about his own experiences with racism as a way of explaining or translating African Americans' frustration to the larger American audience. He also pointed to intraracial violence as a serious problem for young Black boys. In the end, he didn't offer any sweeping policy changes or major pieces of legislation; he saw them as essentially futile, given the kind of remedy needed. Instead, he suggested that the problem of race and racial prejudice would be repaired only through efforts to deal with the anger of young Black boys and the efforts of all Americans to do some serious soul-searching about their own prejudices.[1]

In terms of discursive structure, this had all the ingredients of the best Obama speeches. Known for his rhetorical acumen, Barack Obama has been both lauded and criticized for both his substantive content and his style. There are some components that have become hallmarks of his rhetoric. First, he almost always provides some sort of *personal connection* through anecdotal family history or his lived experiences. Second, he mirrors the *high-minded discourse* of the 1960s civil rights movement or other

unifying historical eras that demonstrate American exceptionalism. This is particularly true in terms of his reliance on quotes
by Martin Luther King Jr. Third, he often serves as a *racial interlocutor* between various groups. Indeed, he spends a good deal of
time translating opposing positions in search of a workable middle
ground. Fourth, he *highlights particular histories* of these groups as
a way of demonstrating shared experiences and the potential for
common ground. He is particularly skilled at equating events that
happen in the same time period but actually represent irreconcilable and conflicting perspectives. Fifth, and last, in his explicit
discussions of race, he points to stereotypes based in beliefs about
African American *cultural pathology*. Obama does some of these
things in some speeches and not others, but they are all quite common and map almost perfectly onto any of his discussions that
involve explicit discussions of race.

The Race Whisperer isn't just about Barack Obama's explicit
race discussions. It is about the multifaceted ways his presidency
has been imbued by race. Making race visible and understanding
the mechanisms through which it is employed is, at times, more
difficult in what is often called the postracial era. Several decades
of research about the process through which race is socially constructed and inculcated into American discourse tells us that most
of our racial understandings are pieced together by what is not
said about race as much by as what is actually verbalized (Roediger
2007; Omi and Winant 1994). George Lipsitz (2006, 1) has said that
"as the unmarked category against which difference is constructed,
whiteness never has to speak its name, never has to acknowledge
its role as an organizing principle in social and cultural relations."
Because the presidency had been exclusive to white males before
Obama was elected, discussions about race and the employment
of racialized rhetoric were framed from the perspective of the

dominant group. There is no guarantee that President Obama will depart from those perspectives, but because he is the first member of a marginalized group to occupy the office, it is particularly important to understand how he uses race in his rhetoric. Examining how Obama uses racial rhetoric to mobilize voters, neutralize opponents and critics, and unsettle or reinforce the contemporary racial order requires an examination of both his explicit and implicit invocation of race and racial ideations. Such an examination explains reactions (moderate and extreme) of supporters and detractors while also illustrating how Americans of many racial and ethnic identities understand racial tropes.

Virtually no conversation in America is devoid of race. This is true for the rhetoric all presidents employ, but it is particularly true for our nation's first Black president. From the historical importance of his election to ways that his election might translate into a different governing style, everything that Barack Obama has done is seen through the lens of the very specific racial history he is making. Indeed, David Tesler and Michael O. Sears (2010, 92) concluded that "any issue Obama takes a public stand on might soon become polarized according to racial dispositions." Thus, to paraphrase Tip O'Neill, all politics regarding Obama is racial.

Barack Obama's presidential candidacy and presidency present a unique opportunity to engage in a discussion about race and politics because of his own multifaceted racial history and the many racial questions that have arisen. The Obama years have highlighted the complexity and sometimes the fluidity of our nation's racial makeup, racial history, racial allegiances, and racial grammar. All of this was highlighted by the death of Trayvon Martin and Obama's reflections on Martin's death. Making that complexity more legible is the primary goal of *The Race Whisperer*. This book looks at how Obama explicitly and implicitly invokes racialized narratives and tropes. The book also examines the impact of those invocations on American politics. As a corollary, it also examines reactions to his speeches that unveil the impact of President Obama's use of racial rhetoric and imagery on the received knowledge of groups. What changes about the presidency when the race of the president changes? What are some of the lessons we can learn about Obama's views of race in America? In what ways does he benefit from or is hampered by engaging in "race talk"? This book relies on a series of case studies that explore how Obama wields racial rhetoric as a political instrument to achieve particular aims such as connecting to specific racial populations or distancing himself from others. It will explore important racialized aspects of both his campaigns and presidency. Before outlining more clearly what I mean by race as a political instrument, it is important to establish the political context in which Obama ran and now governs and the scholarship with which this book engages.

My primary interest is in the way Barack Obama uses racial schemas to galvanize the support of identity groups, what those schemas tell us about his views of race, and how the interactive effects of his implementation and the public's response impacts Black politics. Instead of relying on time-worn tropes regarding race and racial positioning, he has marshaled multiple narratives about his own racial heritage to mobilize support, garner acceptance in multiple communities, and diminish the contentious impact of his race during his candidacies and administrations. In this rhetoric, race does not stop being a collection of socially constructed and experientially meaningful categories. Race is still these things. In addition, however, the narratives Obama tells, his affect as he delivers those narratives, and the references he makes to particular racial identities become political instruments he uses to elicit support for his political goals among citizens. In most campaign rhetoric, race is viewed and discussed in terms of static and intractable categories that politicians use to mobilize or demobilize voters. Barack Obama also tries to influence voting behavior through the use of racial rhetoric. However, his use of racial narratives treats conversations, ideations, and other sentiments toward race as fluid, malleable, and highly susceptible to context. That is, verbal expressions of race are important, but racial understandings are also highly situational, temporally dependent, and performative. Knowing how to connect all these elements in order to use racial language in the most beneficial ways is like understanding which notes on a musical instrument produces the most harmonious sound. Obama's use of race as a political instrument is specific enough to touch the central issues that are most important to individual voters and broad enough to appeal to a wide cross-section of voters. It is interconnected and interactive in a way that requires him to understand ever-changing racial perspectives and preferences and how they might fit together to create a winning electoral coalition. It also avoids extremes so that the concepts he discusses do not go beyond the accepted boundaries of what appears to be fair and unbiased. Like musical instruments, political instruments are played by the performer (e.g., politician, candidate, operative, etc.) in ways that suggest mastery and interpretation of both the instrument and the compositions being played. The "compositions" of interest in this project center on race. President Obama is choosing which compositions to highlight and which to deemphasize. He decides the pace and the tone.

Obama has a much deeper and nuanced understanding of the changing and malleable nature of the racial landscape than previous presidential candidates. This is likely due to a combination of factors that include his membership in a marginalized racial group, his mixed-race heritage, the time he spent abroad, the schools he attended, and the jobs he has held. This allows him, unlike many other politicians, to draw on complex and personal racial narratives in order to appeal to diverse sets of voters. He uses his understanding of these narratives to tap into personal and historical examples that reinforce core positive values of voters and directs the resulting good will toward himself as the designated representative of those values. His audiences hear his version of American history and current events, a version that is not always explicitly racial but is certainly inherently racial, and there is a certain resonance. When Obama is most successful, the narrative he offers does this without seeming to be overly rehearsed or synthetic. There is a sense that these instruments emerge organically from the makeup and mood of the room or the import of the occasion. His ease of transition from one trope to another gives his rhetoric an unbroken quality that renders the movement invisible unless he is addressing a direct question about race. Even on those occasions where he is directly engaging race, his words can be read on multiple levels.

It is also important to understand the nature of choice in instrumentalizing race. Just as a performer would choose not to perform music meant for dancing at a funeral, so Obama must make choices about what tropes are appropriate for a given audience or occasion. There are many racial tropes, both negative and positive, that could be used when speaking to any group. Attentiveness to which ones to prioritize is equally as important as attentiveness to which ones to avoid. This is the work of the race whisperer: not just to revel in sound but to identify the instrument and the composition and to note the consequences of choices. My goal in this book is to outline and render political instruments visible as a way of understanding the process by which politicians are framing their political messages and how ordinary citizens are shaped by those messages.

Deconstructing the Obama Phenomenon

Understanding the context in which a Black candidate emerged as a front-runner for a major political party and subsequently won the presidency of the United States has been a major project of deconstructing what I refer to as the "Obama phenomenon." This terminology serves several rhetorical purposes. First, it points to the tendency to overemphasize the role of personal charisma in Black political success. Erica Edwards's (2012) important work highlights the limits of charisma and cults of personality for bringing about Black progress. Although Obama's achievements loom large and his name is easily listed in the same breath as those of Martin Luther King, W. E. B. Du Bois, and other luminaries, *The Race Whisperer* argues that he uses charisma and his membership status to solidify Black voter loyalty instead of offering policy concessions or promises that would represent real progress toward Black political and social empowerment. As a result, his successful election and presidency becomes the only "legitimate" issue on the Black political agenda, and any discussions or efforts that contradict that goal are derided. Second, the phrase harkens back to Adolph Reed's (1986) now-classic treatise on the 1984 election, *The Jesse Jackson Phenomenon*, which argues that Jackson's run was an attempt to achieve personal electoral and political legitimacy among newly elected Black politicians. Finally, the "Obama phenomenon" is the name of an edited volume about the 2008 election in which scholars dissect every aspect of the historic campaign (Henry, Allen, and Chrisman 2011).

The ascension of Barack Obama to the presidency has been interpreted and reinterpreted many times over in the years since he was elected. Scholars, pundits, and citizens alike have been preoccupied with attempts to understand how he was able to successfully win the Democratic nomination and the White House and what that meant for the changing face of America. Was this an outward rejection of conservative arguments that suggested the browning of America would be its downfall and the only real solution would be to figure out ways to insist that immigrants assimilate to America culture (Huntington 2005)? Had the nation turned a real and significant racial corner in which cross-racial voting would be the order of the day and Blacks in higher office would be accepted as competent leaders? Were Blacks finally at the center of American politics and able to wield their status as the most cohesive Democratic voting bloc in ways that translated into influence over policy outcomes? These are just a few of the questions that have been endlessly debated. Without President Obama's ability to navigate difficult racial waters, there would have been no space and opportunity for any of these discussions. Instead of being seen as a race whisperer, he would be seen as yet another candidate of color running a largely symbolic campaign.

Most of the discussions centered on two main questions. First, there was an enormous interest in whether the election of the first Black president meant the end of racism's stranglehold on American social and political life. If whites could support a Black candidate for the nation's highest office, then surely the vestiges of past notions about Black inferiority must have dissipated.[2] As a result, entire constellations of beliefs and suppositions about race and elections would have to be recalibrated. Second, the candidate himself represented a source of national curiosity. Support for Obama in 2008 wasn't just the election of any Black candidate; it was about the election of this candidate in particular, a candidate who had a rather unorthodox racial story, pristine credentials, and one of the most photogenic political families since the Kennedys. There had been Black presidential candidates before—Chisholm in '72, Jackson in '84 and '88, and Sharpton in '04, for example— but the Democratic nomination remained elusive for Blacks until Obama (Sinclair-Chapman and Price 2008). His success rested in part on his ability to position himself as both an African American insider and as somehow more than that. Many described it as an ability to transcend race.

Barack Obama as a political character and the persona shaped by his campaign elicited tremendous cross-racial appeal. He helped himself quite a bit with the publication of two successful biographies, *Dreams from My Father* (2004b) and *The Audacity of Hope* (2008a).[3] Both books were bestsellers and helped introduce the public to his background and political development. What is now a very familiar story was mostly unknown in 2007. He was born to a white American mother and a Kenyan father, both of whom were students in Hawaii. Eventually his father moved back to Kenya and Obama was raised by his single mother with the help of her parents. He also lived abroad during his childhood with his mother and Indonesian stepfather. He attended some of the best schools in the country, including Columbia and Harvard. His first job after college was as a community organizer in Chicago, and after leaving for law school he returned to that city. There he married Michelle Robinson and fathered two daughters. His political aspirations took him quickly from the Illinois statehouse to the U.S. Senate to the White House. He acquired diverse experiences during this life history that would resonate with many voter constituencies.

Barack Obama began framing his story on the national stage during the 2004 Democratic National Convention. In his speech there, Obama, a relative political unknown, devoted a significant amount of time to his personal narrative. He presented this narrative not as a way to introduce himself personally; rather, he presented himself as a personification of the American dream: his life experience embodied the values enshrined by the founders of the nation. Most important, he framed his narrative as universal (and thus raceless). He told his audience at the convention and the national audience across the airwaves that his experience was "a part of the larger American story . . . and in no other country on earth, is [this] story even possible" (Obama 2004a).

Some scholars pointed to Obama's unorthodox lineage in interesting and varied ways. They argued that his lack of connection to descendants of slaves in the American South meant that the majority of African Americans would have trouble identifying with him (Walters 2007; Williams 2004). Alternatively, some argued that whites might see him as exceptional or somehow different from other Blacks and, consequently, more attractive to white voters. Obama walked a difficult tightrope that involved demonstrating the right amount of authenticity and connection to the Black community without being seen as a racial threat by whites (Squires and Jackson 2010). Skillfully changing one's style and rhetoric for particular audiences without being seen as a panderer is the singular talent of the race whisperer. In fact, the invisibility of that shift is the key to its success. This ability demonstrates a racial literacy that requires an understanding of how multiple and at times competing racial groups discuss and receive political messages. Moreover, it demonstrates a capacity to use that knowledge in the heat of political campaigns, where the context in which candidates find themselves at any given moment is constantly changing.

Obama was also able to capitalize on "W fatigue." George W. Bush's popularity had waned considerably due to dissatisfaction with the progress of the War on Terror and the rapidly sinking economy. Fred Greenstein (2009) argues that the two factors that were most impactful in Obama's victory were dissatisfaction with Bush and the economic downturn that happened on Bush's watch. While these surely played a part, this argument provides very little attention to or insight into why or how non-Black Americans were able to overcome centuries of history and voting behavior to elect the first Black president. He was clearly able to tap into greater support among "racial liberals" than either previous Black candidates or his white contemporaries (Tesler and Sears 2010).

Obama's campaign was innovative on many fronts. It developed a sophisticated machine that used new media and social networking tools to disseminate information, recruit volunteers, and mobilize voters. Using this new technology, Obama amassed record campaign funds from sources that were more varied than in any other campaign in history. His 2008 campaign raised well over $700 million dollars, nearly 90 percent of which came from individual contributions (OpenSecrets.org, n.d.). Throughout the election season, the Obama campaign boasted about the amount of money it raised from small and first-time donors and suggested that this phenomenon signaled a groundswell of grassroots support for his candidacy. The campaign's fund-raising patterns signaled that Obama was tapping into members of new and often-overlooked constituencies who shared his vision for the future. He quoted Gandhi and King but he also quoted Jay-Z and Beyoncé. He was endorsed by both established political families and by actors and actresses. The demand for seats at his speech at the 2008 Democratic National Convention was so great that the site was moved from the Denver Convention Center to Mile High Stadium, where the NFL's Denver Broncos played.

By the general election in November 2008, Obama had achieved rock-star status that was only magnified by the fact that a battalion of celebrities was actively campaigning for him. In addition, young voters were attracted to his story and turned out heavily to volunteer for his campaign and vote for him in the election. In 2008, turnout among young voters increased significantly; Barack Obama received nearly 70 percent of votes of those under thirty. According to the Pew Research Center, young voters attended more campaign events and donated more money in 2008 than they had in previous years. A major factor may have been that many more youth said they had been contacted by the Obama campaign; nearly a quarter of all youth said they had been contacted either in person or by phone by someone from the Obama campaign (Keeter, Horowitz, and Tyson 2008). Obama won the presidency with 53 percent of the popular vote and a solid majority among women, first-time voters, African Americans, Latinos, and Asians.

African Americans played a key role in the 2008 election. They were a pivotal Democratic voting bloc in southern states, where whites had largely abandoned the Democratic Party. As states continued to push their primaries to earlier dates in the election season, South Carolina became an important test of Obama's staying power after his unexpected defeat in New Hampshire. African Americans constituted a majority of Democratic voters in South Carolina, and a third of these voters were African American women (Seelye 2008b). Though prior to that primary Blacks had split their support between Obama and Hillary Clinton, Obama won South Carolina with a 55 percent majority.[4] Blacks' decision to support Obama gave him a large share of the vote in the Democratic primary and allowed him to remain competitive against Hillary Clinton. It is no secret that Blacks consistently support the Democratic Party in general elections. However, unlike other presidential candidates, Obama received a near-unanimous endorsement from African Americans by garnering 96 percent of the Black vote.[5] Moreover, for the first time ever, African American women had the highest turnout rate of all groups (Lopez and Taylor 2009). African Americans viewed this election as an important historical moment and were excited about the prospect of voting for the first Black president.

Much of the analysis of Obama's 2008 victory rests on a static view of race. That is, it treats race as a set of defined categories in which individuals hold membership and assumes that this membership impacts their worldview. Analysts focused on questions related to the racial identity of voters and candidates and how these identities have come to reflect certain predictable political outcomes. Thus, the story of the 2008 election essentially became a process of deconstructing and explaining aberrant behavior. Analysts asked how the actors behaved differently and why. There was special interest, for instance, in how Obama differed from other Black candidates, other Democratic candidates, and his Republican opponents (Bai 2008; Remnick 2008). Even his authenticity as an African American was questioned, given his biracial heritage, and some seemed to argue that he was so different from other candidates that comparisons were almost irrelevant (Seelye 2008a; Remnick 2008). There were also discussions about white support for a Black candidate over a white female candidate (Seelye 2008a; Nagourney 2006). Others were attentive to how other marginalized groups made choices about whether or not to support Obama (e.g., Latinos, members of the LGBT community, and, to some extent, Asian Americans [Hornick 2008; Cullen 2008; Baim 2010]).

Baodong Liu (2010, 8) argues that the fundamental key to Obama's victory was his ability to mobilize a "minimum winning coalition" composed of a high proportion of minority voters and a low proportion of white voters. He argues that winning the presidency requires candidates to gain the support of a large majority of either minorities or whites and some minimum of the other. Building a base of support premised on this simple calculation actually required a sound strategy and an enormous amount of effort to build. Obama and his election team proved to be powerfully skilled at this. They successfully crafted a masterful personal narrative that was simultaneously universal and specific. His personal story was so unorthodox that he was able to connect to parts of many voters' life experiences but wholly to almost no one. Obama was also able to capitalize on Bush's unpopularity and on an election machine that was tied into and understood the power of social media in contemporary elections. He was able to amass support across a wide cross-section of Americans and successfully corral them under one campaign umbrella, in large part due to his ability to deploy personal racial narratives.

Scholars have attempted to outline the electoral innovations that contributed to Obama's success. Valeria Sinclair-Chapman and I (2008) have pointed to several unique racial features of the 2008 election. An important departure from previous elections was the Obama campaign's use of white surrogates such as campaign operatives, party officials, and Democratic officeholders to combat attempts to negatively insert race into the presidential campaign. Obama's Senate colleagues such as Claire McCaskill (D-MO) and Amy Klobuchar (D-MN) appeared on nightly news shows to discredit those who attempted to use implicit racial messages to undermine Obama's campaign. Whites speaking against racist campaign tactics signaled the Democratic Party's turn toward a proactive stance toward racial issues; previously the party had intentionally avoided conversations about race. In addition, Senator Ted Kennedy (D-MA) openly discussed how he was persuaded to endorse Obama because he believed that the Democratic primaries were becoming too divisive as a result of the Clintons' insertions of implicit racial messages (Zeleny and Hulse 2008). Dan Balz and Haynes Johnson (2009) have noted that "for Kennedy, the injection of race into the campaign was hurting both candidates and alienating the party's African American base." Beyond the support of elite whites, Obama made significant headway with other white voters. He received a higher share of white votes in 2008 than Bill Clinton, Al Gore, or John Kerry had done in previous presidential elections (Cobb 2010).

There were many obstacles related to both Blacks' and non-Blacks' expectations of Black politicians. The blustery style of early Black mayors who positioned themselves as adversaries to white city government was unworkable for those Black politicians who wanted to attain higher political office. Thus, President Obama had to carefully craft an image that both resonated with Blacks because of their critical importance to the Democratic electoral coalition and attracted non-Black voters. He had to present a form of Blackness that would secure a cross-section of support. He could not be too angry or aggressive, and he could not take controversial (or any definitive) racial stances or hint at any potential bias toward his own racial group. In addition, he needed to connect with voters beyond obvious phenotypical differences. He also needed Black voters not to push him too hard on racial questions that might repel non-Black voters.

Pundits continually noted that (presumably unlike other Black candidates) Obama was not angry. Thus, he was potentially more appealing to white voters. Frank Rudy Cooper (2008, 636) went so far as to label him the nation's first "unisex president" because "Obama's calmness has roots in the general need of Black men to be non-threatening to achieve mainstream success." Thus, his failure to adhere to societal norms of masculinity mostly regarding anger and aggression made his candidacy different from other male candidates. Many of the characteristics that Obama was most praised for implicitly signaled the differences between him and other Blacks. He was Black but not like other Blacks and not like other categories of famous Black men, such as athletes, rappers, and actors. All of these factors taken together seemingly provided a new racial context for white voters, but these were potentially less salient factors for African American voters.

If Obama was to win, it was necessary that Blacks not require too much of him. Conversations in which constituencies hash out demands with prospective politicians often force the politicians to articulate positions and policy goals. Those articulations are revealing, both to the group whose support is being courted and to other groups. Fred Harris's (2012) *The Price of the Ticket* suggests that African Americans were willing to overlook many things about Obama, both during and after the 2008 election. He calls it a "wink-and-nod" agreement that "entails black voters giving race-neutral black politicians a pass on discussion about racial inequality in exchange for the candidates' successful elevation to high-profile political offices" (139). African Americans understood the difficult road Obama had to travel and gave him implicit permission to avoid racial issues that might derail his chance of election. In a poignant quote, an African American woman told *The Washington Post* that "'we can be black all day' after the election. . . . 'We've got to get there first'" (Holmes 2008). While African Americans were well aware of the sacrifice they were making, it is unclear if most understood that this campaign bargain would follow the president into the White House. The goal seemed to be getting Obama elected by any means necessary; there was never a negotiation of post-election expectations. *The Race Whisperer* analyzes the implicit nods that Harris points to and extends the analysis to include racial cues that target other racial groups. Melissa Harris-Perry (2011, 272) put forth a similar idea with a more race-neutral tone by arguing that the president was practicing a "'green screen' political strategy" in which "Barack Obama hoped to place himself in front of a blank space onto which Americans could project their own identities, political goals, and national hopes." Like other groups, Blacks projected their beliefs onto him, but unlike some groups with whom the Candidate Obama met and made promises to, these projections were made without explicit promises. Obama remained free of specific obligations to his community of origin.

The success of the campaign pivoted on Obama's ability to play up universal messages that promote cross-racial appeal. He relied on race-neutral themes or themes related to aspects of African American history that have become a part of America's universal understanding of itself. I argue later in *The Race Whisperer* that so-called postracial rhetoric is decidedly not race neutral and instead reinforces the existing racial order. Avoiding postracial arguments, Enid Logan (2011, 8), who analyzes newspaper coverage of the 2008 election, suggests that race and its role in American politics differed that year from the past. She argues that the outcome was attributable to the fact that Obama offered an "appealing, carefully moderated version of Blackness that a majority of the electorate readily consumed." Her arguments suggest that this did not diminish the impact of race in the election, but it did restrict the terms of racial conversations to conciliatory concepts instead of those that might elicit hostility or conflict. She also notes a greater emphasis on the import of a Black president and less attentiveness to the possibility of a woman president leading up to the election. In light of Logan's findings, it is less surprising that Donald Kinder and Allison Dale-Riddle (2012) found that while racial group solidarity influenced voters' choices significantly, the same was not true for gender identity. However, Obama's campaign staff noted that they rarely discussed his race in the campaign (Parks and Rachlinsky 2009, 230). If this is true, it may have been the only space where that was the case because everyone else discussed it continuously. As William Jelani Cobb (2010, 160) astutely notes, however, "the Achilles heel of the 'postracial' politician, to the extent that such a thing exists, is that there are consistent clockwork moments of racial outrage that level-headed appeals for calm can't address." Cobb's argument is particularly prescient given the distinctly racial tenor of many of the events in the latter half of Obama's second term.

Racist Appeals, Racial Appeals, and Obama Appeals

In *The Race Whisperer*, I argue that Barack Obama is uniquely situated to tap into multiple racial appeals. For him, access to particular racial appeals is not determined by membership in specific and mutually exclusive groups. He is able to make authentic and politically useful connections to multiple groups, including whiteness, without actually being white. Indeed, he is able to wield racial appeals as instruments of mobilization to bring together diverse and divergent groups (particularly when it comes to histories and policy positions). A significant portion of this ability stems from his capacity to tailor his biography to establish powerful connections with many groups. His multiracial background, his experiences living abroad, his Ivy League education, and his organizing skills all provide source material for bold and genuine claims to membership across and among identities and categories. In this way, he is able to tap into narratives of Blackness, whiteness, migration, and other things with a good amount of credibility. This book examines how he is able to do this. His ability to tap into important and wide-ranging cultural scripts all candidates use presents a new challenge to our understanding of race in campaigns, in elections, and in Black politics. Through an analysis of his own words, news reportage, and case studies, *The Race Whisperer* highlights the myriad ways he instrumentalizes racial appeals and the resulting implications for our understanding of Barack Obama's racial legacy and the future of Black politics.

Before moving to concrete examples of Obama's use of race and racial appeals, it is important to provide some background about the role of racial imagery in mobilizing or demobilizing a segment of the electorate. African Americans have embodied whites' racial fears about crime, welfare, and other national problems. These fears have crystalized during elections around specific Black people who typified these problems; examples include Willie Horton, Sistah Souljah, and Jeremiah Wright.

On both sides of the aisle, we see the use of racial appeals to garner white support. In the post–civil rights era, the two major parties have become racially polarized. Blacks and other minorities have become the cornerstone of the Democratic voting coalition, while Republicans have had enormous electoral success mostly through the support of white voters. Party appeals and campaign strategies are further complicated by the fact that race-neutral language, at least in public, is de rigueur and most Americans see explicitly racial appeals that highlight or advocate racial balkanization as out of place. Understanding that parties are dividing along "racial cleavages," Tali Mendelberg's (2001, 7) *The Race Card* investigates the use of racial messaging in contemporary campaigns. She argues that politicians have come to rely on implicit messages because they allow politicians to "convey racial messages implicitly when two contradictory conditions hold: (1) they wish to avoid violation the norms of racially equality, and (2) they face incentives to mobilize racially resentful white voters." That is, they want to mobilize white voters using problematic racial tropes but do not want to be seen as doing so. Hence, the deployment of implicit racial messages has become a mainstay of American campaigning.

Mendelberg's work is instructive because it demonstrates how racial messages can be used to sway voters regardless of their level of awareness of the message. This makes implicit racial messages successful but also dangerously able to erode the gains of the civil rights era. Potential voters subconsciously process racial messages without the benefit of more conscious filters that mediate social norms and principles. Interestingly, she finds that much of the power of these attacks can be diminished when the racist message and its intent is exposed. Once the way racial messages are used is pointed out, they become less powerful. Thus, making the message plain decreases its impact on most white voters.[6]

During the 1988 presidential election, the Republican Party sought to show American voters that the Democratic nominee, Michael Dukakis, was a Massachusetts liberal who was soft on crime. They used a commercial that showed a menacing mugshot of an African American man, William "Willie" Horton, a felon who had committed murder and rape while out of jail on a furlough program. The commercial showed prisoners walking out of prison through a revolving door to suggest that they were coming and going as they pleased. Many accused the Bush campaign of running a racist commercial that played on whites' fears about crime and especially about Black men and sexual depravity (Dowd 1988).

In 1992, presidential candidate Bill Clinton emerged as the Democratic front-runner, but after successive Republican presidents, he and other members of the conservative wing of the Democratic Party outlined a path to a successful Democratic presidency. Sistah Souljah was a member of the rap group Public Enemy who made a comment about "killing white people" after the Los Angeles riots (Mills 1992). Not long after, she was invited to a meeting convened by Jesse Jackson's Operation PUSH/Rainbow Coalition. When a reporter asked Clinton what he thought about that, he used the moment to reprimand Jesse Jackson for including her. This became known as "the Sista Souljah moment" because it was an opportunity for Clinton to demonstrate that he was not afraid to challenge the Black community and its leaders (Smith 1996).

Video footage of a sermon shortly after September 11th showed Jeremiah Wright declaring that America had gotten what it deserved because of its problematic foreign policy decisions. The footage was part of a longer discussion that had been spliced together by a blogger. But the damage of the sound-bite was undeniable—as was Wright's close connection to the Obamas. Reverend Wright had performed the wedding ceremony of Barack and Michelle Obama and had baptized his two daughters. By Obama's own admission, the title of his second book, *The Audacity of Hope* (2008a), was inspired by one of Wright's sermons. Obama at first said he was not present when Wright made the statements about September 11th. However, as additional controversial statements Wright had made were uncovered, it became more difficult for him to claim that he was unaware of Wright's positions. Eventually Obama and his family resigned their membership from his church, but that was not enough to quell debate over this issue.

These names have all become familiar in political circles because of the way their caricatured images have been used to invoke racialized thinking among the American electorate. In all three cases, the individual is neither the object nor the target of the discussion; instead, they are used as rhetorical weapons to strike fear into the hearts of white voters who might be persuaded to vote for a Democratic candidate. They are not necessarily known for what they have done or who they really are. On the contrary, we know the names mostly for what they have come to symbolize in American politics and because of the role of racial images, especially the images of African Americans, in politics. Indeed, outside of the recent case of Jeremiah Wright, most people probably could not provide the details of how these names came to have so much public resonance, yet many can recall emotions associated with hearing these names invoked in public. There is something about them that we now understand to be larger than their personal stories. When major political candidates are forced to deal with controversial issues related to some aspect of their personal identity or when they make difficult choices about who they will continue to associate with, reporters and pundits frequently ask whether or not this is the candidate's Sistah Souljah moment. Her name has been transformed into an adjective that suggests at the very least difficulties or problems in a campaign. The people listed above share the common distinction of having had their images used in electioneering in an attempt to exploit or amplify white fears using certain "kinds" of Blacks as a proxy for why we should fear all Blacks, even Black and Black-aligned political candidates.

Since the mass introduction of African Americans into the electorate in the mid-1960s, candidates for the Democratic and Republican parties have experimented with various ways to use racial thinking to achieve desired results in elections (Frymer 1999; Carmines and Stimson 1989). Republicans have appealed to military hawks, religious conservatives, and disaffected whites (particularly men) who fled the Democratic Party during the civil rights and post–civil rights eras. This was accomplished with a hard push to the political right within the party, but these efforts were augmented by a vote-gathering strategy that involved deploying negative racial imagery of African Americans. Regardless of content, these strategies have relied heavily on the unsubstantiated fears of whites regarding Black crime, Black hostility toward whites, affirmative action programs, and federal public assistance programs. The underlying message of all these topics is that the government coddles the undeserving poor and racial minorities (Philpot 2007; Fauntroy 2006). One can trace these initial efforts back to incidents such as Ronald Reagan's decision to give a speech about states' rights, the justification for southern segregation, in Philadelphia, Mississippi, the town where Civil Rights movement martyrs Schwerner, Chaney, and Goodman were slaughtered by agents of white resistance using states' rights as their justification. Or Reagan's repeated invocation of the mythical welfare queen who was getting rich on government benefits (Hancock 2004). Other examples of such efforts include the famous "white hands" commercial run by white Republican Jesse Helms in a senatorial election against Black Democrat Harvey Gantt (Reeves 1997). In this now (in)famous commercial, a camera closes in tightly on the arm and hand of a white man in a flannel shirt holding a piece of paper that is clearly a rejection letter. Simultaneously, a narrator offers a monologue about the man not being able to get a job because of racial quotas. Then the camera cuts to a picture of Gantt and Massachusetts senator Ted Kennedy and says that they both support quotas. The use of William "Willie" Horton's image to demonstrate Michael Dukakis's softness on crime is another example. Anonymous flyers appeared in South Carolina in 2004 suggesting that John McCain was the father of an illegitimate Black child, when in fact he had adopted a dark-skinned Bangladeshi child many years before (Steinhauer 2007). These are just a few of the most egregious examples of racial pandering on the part of Republican candidates and their strategists.

These examples are not aberrations; they indicate a larger pattern that is part and parcel of the resurgence of the Republican Party. Indeed, new information continues to emerge about the sentiments of Republican Party strategists and their views on the use of racially prejudicial thinking. Lee Atwater, probably the most important electoral strategist in modern campaigning and the mastermind behind the Horton ad, spoke very clearly about the problem with socially desirable or politically correct mandates against overt racism. In an audio recording released in 2012 for the first time, Atwater can be heard discussing race and racism as it relates to political campaigning. Atwater says,

> You start out in 1954 by saying, "Nigger, nigger, nigger." By 1968 you can't say "nigger"—that hurts you, backfires. So you say stuff like, uh, forced busing, states' rights, and all that stuff, and you're getting abstract. Now you're talking about cutting taxes, and all these things you're talking about are totally economic things and a by-product of them is, blacks getting hurt worse than whites. (Herbert 2005; also quoted in Perlstein 2012)

Taken from a 1981 interview, this quote was originally published as an unattributed quote. It has only recently been published as an attributed comment. The quote demonstrates the purposeful way that members of the political right sought to maintain an electoral stronghold among whites in the post–civil rights era.

While members of the Democratic Party have not engaged in racially hostile campaigning in the same manner as the Republican Party, they are by no means exempt from this discussion. At the same time that the Republicans have engaged in actively hostile strategies against Democrats because of their associations with Blacks, Democrats have done as much as possible to avoid being seen as the party of Blacks and other minorities. Carmines and Stimson (1989) outline clearly how the Democratic Party came to be associated with African Americans, mostly because of their bold positions on civil rights in the 1960s. As a reward for Democrats' support for civil rights goals, when Blacks gained increased access to the ballot they consistently voted for Democratic candidates. African American party loyalty has resulted in a strong cadre of Black elected officials in the federal and state legislatures and at the local level, but until 2008 this had not translated into representation at the presidential level.

Neither Democrats nor Republicans have made rewarding Black voter loyalty a priority. In contrast, both parties have focused on the preferences of white voters.[7] White voters, it was believed, were reluctant to vote for Democratic Party candidates for two interrelated reasons that implicate Blacks and other minorities. First, Democrats were seen as the party of big government and financial irresponsibility, largely because of their support for major social programs stemming from the War on Poverty and other redistributive programs such as affirmative action. Though they are not the largest recipients of welfare benefits (whites, in fact, are) or affirmative action opportunities (white women are), the face of both of these efforts remains Black (Gilens 1999; Bobo 1998). Welfare and affirmative action programs are overwhelmingly associated with Blacks and are consistently viewed as being exploited by the undeserving poor. Second, because of Democrats' strong position on civil rights and long-standing Black voter loyalty, the Democratic Party is viewed as the party of minorities in general and Blacks specifically (Smith 1996; Carmines and Stimson 1989). Whites, to extend the argument Smith and Carmines and Stimson made, see their interests as being in conflict with those of minorities; consequently, white voters cannot or will not support the same party or candidate as minority voters. According to Ian Haney López (2014), this division has been nurtured through the use of implicit racial cues that distract middle-class whites from their true interests and advance the goals of the wealthiest few, using what he calls "dog whistle politics."

Bill Clinton's 1992 campaign best illustrates the nature of this relationship. He was very popular with Black voters. He was generally seen as someone who was comfortable around large groups of African Americans; in fact, he made a special appearance on the popular late-night program *The Arsenio Hall Show* to play jazz saxophone. He was completely at ease in Black church pulpits, at soul food restaurants, and at other predominantly Black venues. Indeed, the media loved to comment on his popularity among African Americans. As a key member of the centrist Democratic Leadership Council, Clinton also felt the need to demonstrate that unlike previous Democrats, he was not soft on crime *or* specifically beholden to any part of the Democratic voting coalition.[8] Thus, he engaged in two activities that illustrate the complexity of relations between Blacks and Democrats. First, he very publicly left the campaign trail in 1992 to oversee the execution of Ricky Ray Rector, a mentally disabled African American man convicted of murdering a police officer (Bright 1995; Applebome 1992).[9] The act was meant to demonstrate that he was tough on crime and to position him in opposition to previous Democratic candidates. The second example is the original Sistah Souljah moment discussed earlier.

Though Mendelberg calls such messages implicit racial messages because they mobilize voters through veiled references to race, the messages she examines can also be called racist messages. In more recent elections, the number of political issues that can be used to stir up public fears have grown not declined. As a consequence, candidates can now exploit old fears related to patriotism and citizenship and new ones related to terrorism. Charlton McIlwain and Stephen M. Caliendo (2011, 16) expand the meaning of racial appeals to include more than just appeals with racist content. They astutely point out that "all racist appeals are racial, but not all racial appeals are racist." By broadening the definition of racial appeals and distinguishing between racial appeals and racist appeals, they expand the universe of racial appeals and the types of candidates who are able to access these appeals as a campaign tool. Hence, racial appeals can be racist or merely discuss racial issues, and they can be implicit or explicit.

Mendelberg examines Republican efforts exclusively because she focuses on the use of implicitly racist messages. McIlwain and Caliendo's (2011, 16) intervention broadens the scope of what constitutes a racial appeal to include any instance of candidates who invoke racial thinking during the course of a campaign. Racial appeals can be used by all races, and their content is not necessarily anti-minority. African American and Latino candidates can use racial appeals just as easily as white candidates, and racial appeals can be based on divisive sentiments as easily as racially inclusive messages. McIlwain and Caliendo's most innovative contribution to the literature on racial appeals stems from their work on how and why candidates of color use racial appeals (35–39). They find that minority candidates use these appeals to perform a *racial inoculation* function through narratives that counteract prevailing stereotypes, suggest *racial authenticity*, and operate as a *racial defense* against racist appeals. All of these functions are derived from the need of minority candidates to combat entrenched racial prejudice among white voters and demonstrate a racial connection to minority voters, particularly members of their own group. It reflects a need to balance an appropriate combination of racial authenticity and distance from the stereotypes associated with a group.

Previous research regarding how candidates access, devise, and deploy racial appeals remains fairly static. The terrain on which these candidates must vie for office is one in which white voters must overcome their conscious and subconscious negative perceptions of people of color generally and candidates of color specifically. White candidates use one set of appeals for white voters and another, when necessary, for racial minorities. Alternatively, Blacks, Latinos, and other minority candidates have one set of racial appeals for white voters and others for minority voters. For Mendelberg, white candidates use racist racial appeals to exploit white voters' fears about Blacks and as a complement to appeals to patriotism and the American creed that serve as a proxy for whiteness. For McIlwain and Caliendo, white candidates do all of these same things and candidates of color try to counter white voters' anti-minority sentiments and demonstrate in-group connections. In both estimations there is no room for overlap in the kinds of appeals whites and non-whites can make and the motivations for using particular appeals. Barack Obama challenges this assertion through the style and content of his engagement with race.

A Note about Intent

In political discussions there is always a temptation to attach cynical and even sinister motives to the behavior and words of political actors and politicians. For at least four decades, levels of American political trust have been plummeting, largely because of continuous political scandals brought on by the ethical lapses of politicians. Cynicism has become the zeitgeist of American political culture. For African Americans, political trust has never been particularly high (Nunnally 2012). They have had very few reasons to trust politicians and very few presidencies have deserved their trust. For both Blacks and non-Blacks, Obama campaigned as an alternative to cynicism by focusing on his embodiment of hope about many American ills. He in turn was rewarded for that with votes from various groups, especially from Blacks and other racial minorities and youth of all races. It is difficult to say (and I am not prepared to do so) that his focus on hope and the future was a cynical attempt to dupe these groups in order to achieve his electoral goals.

America is a racially polarized nation that requires a cross-racial voting coalition if a candidate is to win high office. This is a difficult line to walk for any politician. For an African American politician, whose presence alone can invoke racial thinking, it is almost impossible. So it is true, as Obama has said himself many times, that he doesn't have to mention that he is Black because everyone in the room sees and understands that it matters. Whether he talks about race or not, it is the elephant in the room. However, how he talks about race can vary a great deal. He understands better than most the cleavages in American social and political life. Consequently, when he emphasizes a particular perspective, it is hard not to believe that it was intentional. This is also true because he is credited with writing many of his own speeches and has taken sole credit for both his 2008 speech on race, "A More Perfect Union," and his comments on Trayvon Martin. It becomes difficult to say that he isn't speaking with particular audiences in mind and with a specific expectation about how the content will be received by those audiences.

After having watched him closely and having read most things published about him in the last six or seven years, I believe that he is quite intentional in most of his public actions. I also agree with David Mayhew (2004), who insists that the primary goal of politicians is to be elected. In American presidential elections, the guaranteed formula for that in the post–civil rights era has been to attract as many white voters as possible, and candidates accomplish this mostly through distancing themselves from Blacks and other minorities. Democratic candidates do their best to achieve this without alienating minorities. For Republicans, minority sentiments don't really matter. For Black candidates, this is trickier; they cannot distance themselves from their own Blackness. They can, however, engage in rhetoric that demonstrates social distance from their own group or refrain from engaging in race talk at all. Obama has done a combination of both. He could not have been elected otherwise.

The goal here is not to punish (or reward) Barack Obama for being a politician. Rather, the goal is to explore the impact of race and race talk coming from the White House when a Black person is standing at the microphone and saying the words. I argue throughout *The Race Whisperer* that real, and sometime troubling, consequences result from his words for the racial group to which he claims membership. I do not cast Barack Obama as either a monster or a hero. Like the ability of the character Robert Redford played in the 1998 film *The Horse Whisperer* to understand the tone, words, and treatment a horse needs to be calmed and then provide that horse with what it needs to get the desired result, Barack Obama is a model "race whisperer." He sees how race works in America and with a great amount of flexibility (as demonstrated in this book) tailors his racial grammar to a specific community and achieves a desired goal. Like Redford's character, Obama is not bombastic; he doesn't gain the obedience of supporters through loud aggression. Instead, he uses calmness, rationality, and patience to convince potential supporters to follow him.

Chapter Overview

The first chapter, "Barack Obama and Black Blame: Authenticity, Audience, and Audaciousness," examines a recurring trope of personal responsibility Barack Obama used during the 2008 campaign that he specifically reserved for Black audiences. This trope is best characterized as moral lectures that both chastised and instructed African Americans on issues ranging from being better parents to being more engaged citizens. Throughout the campaign and since that time, he has used this imagery when he is giving speeches to Black audiences. However, because of his status as president, these speeches have been broadcast beyond Black audiences. As much as he appears to be talking to Blacks, given the makeup of those in the audiences for these speeches, a significant non-Black audience is also listening and taking the measure of his words. In this chapter, I analyze Obama's use of the trope of personal responsibility in an attempt to glean its utility for his campaign, the impact of who the audience was and where he gave such speeches (through an examination of his use of quasi-safe spaces), and the larger impact of this trope.

Chapter 2, "Barack Obama, Patton's Army, and Patriotic Whiteness," explores Obama's reliance on his personal narrative to access patriotic tropes that are usually exclusively reserved for white candidates. Obama's reference to his grandfather's service in World War II as a soldier in Patton's army is not without racial histories and complications. The military has a long history of racial segregation and marginalization that prevented African American soldiers from full participation in all aspects of war, including many that we now memorialize as the most patriotic. Thus, the Black veteran's quest for recognition of service has been a much more difficult journey than that of the white veteran. By looking at these differing experiences and locating Obama's invocation of this historical moment, we see a clear example of the way he can access whiteness in ways that most Black candidates could not.

Chapter 3, "Barack Obama's More Perfect Union," turns to the role of whiteness in understanding the racial implications of Obama's candidacy and presidency. This chapter focuses on Obama's "A More Perfect Union" speech, which is his only formal articulation of his perceptions of American race relations. I argue that in this speech, Obama positions himself as a new Black politician in the same way that third-wave feminists see themselves as different and in many waves more evolved type of feminists. Using critiques of third-wave feminist theorizing and its underlying reification of whiteness, I analyze similar tendencies in Obama's speech. Ultimately I argue that Obama's speech fails to do the work of changing intractable views because it largely does not recognize or resolve important cleavages. In fact, there are instances where his words work to shore up and solidify those cleavages.

In chapter 4, "An Officer and Two Gentlemen: The Great Beer Summit of 2009," I look at the well-worn ground of the relations between African Americans and law enforcement through the lens of the now-famous "Beer Summit" with Henry Louis Gates Jr. that Barack Obama convened in the White House Rose Garden in 2009. This chapter attempts to answer the question: What happens when Barack Obama defends African Americans from the nation's largest bully pulpit? The Gates controversy is interesting because it fits so neatly with the issues of property rights and sovereignty over one's home that conservatives and libertarians are so wont to defend. Despite the obvious ideological overlap, the incident ignited a difficult dialogue about the presidency, citizens, and policing that was marked by race despite most commentators' reluctance to frame it that way. Commonly referred to as a "teachable moment" or an opportunity for the first Black president to bridge the gap of racial understanding among Americans, the lessons learned tell us more about the continuing and consistent nature of that gap rather than the architecture of whatever bridge is capable of crossing it.

I conclude this book by discussing the nature of belonging for African Americans in society and politics. What are the tradeoffs that African Americans have to make to be seen as citizens who belong in the land of their birth? To a great extent, Obama's racial gymnastics were all done to help Americans believe he had the skills and character needed to inhabit the nation's highest office. I also offer a discussion of the innovations and limitations of the Obama model, both for future candidates and as a path to Black empowerment. I argue that Black voters' unconditional support for Obama limited their ability to make group demands (during and after the campaign) of the federal government and its most important spokesperson and policy leader.

1

Barack Obama and Black Blame

Authenticity, Audience, and Audaciousness

Barack Obama's relationship to the Black community is most often treated as fairly straightforward. There was an immeasurable amount of pride in light of his election to the presidency, and the celebration of the moment was felt even by detractors within the community. Photographs of Obama and his family are displayed in Black homes next to photos of beloved grandmothers, nieces, and other kin. His victory, without doubt, was a collective accomplishment that represented forward progress for the entire race.

In the full glow of this historic moment, there was one aspect of that relationship that for many reasons was overlooked. Barack Obama continuously engaged in public excoriations of African Americans and behaviors they engage in that he deems destructive and unsatisfactory. On many occasions and in front of audiences large and small, he mixed forthright campaigning with moral invectives about what members of his racial community should be doing to achieve equality. These were targeted comments that were reserved for Black audiences and used tropes specific to the Black community that were largely unchecked by anyone until well into his second term as president. Taken less seriously in 2008 by the media and the Obama campaign was an unplanned public admonition by Jesse Jackson, who made what he thought was an off-camera remark about Barack Obama "talking down to Black people."[1] It was discarded as a single critique by someone who felt marginalized in a campaign that owed a great debt to Jackson's unsuccessful bids in the 1980s. Interestingly, it also proved beneficial to Obama, who was able to demonstrate another contrast between himself and the Jesse Jackson types of the Black community. Jackson had inadvertently set Obama up for his own Sista Souljah moment wherein the Democratic presidential nominee could distance himself from a person whose image continues to be a racial flashpoint in the minds of many Americans.

Obama consistently employs narratives based on the determinacy of individual choice and personal responsibility rather than on structural impediments to Black equality. I am not arguing that the message is new. It has quite a long trajectory in some schools of African American political thought and American democratic ideals. The interesting question that his engagement raises is how he is able to use fairly damning language that would be viewed as problematic coming from other national candidates with very few consequences for such an extended period. Navigating this kind of difficult territory is the purview of the race whisperer. He steps into public debates within the Black community, arguing that Blacks make poor choices that ultimately block them from the real progress they have been seeking for generations. However, because of the context in which he makes these arguments, he is rarely critiqued for it.

Just a few short years earlier, when Bill Cosby made similar kinds of arguments, there was both support for and critique of what he said. This has not been the case for Obama. He has been able to make negative claims about Black people (especially poor Blacks) while maintaining the support of the African American community and without being seen as a race candidate by whites. I argue that this was accomplished through his nuanced understanding of the role context and audience plays in shaping how messages will be received by various audiences.

This chapter is divided into three parts that explore the process by which Obama uses racial rhetoric. First, I discuss an important paradox that emerged during Obama's initial presidential candidacy. He ran as a deracialized candidate and intentionally avoided racial questions except in two cases: when he was directly questioned and when he was engaging in Black blame. In this chapter, I take up the latter situation. Second, I use his own words to demonstrate the ways he relies on Black blame to undergird his explanations of and remedies for Black problems. Last, I make claims about the importance of context in explaining how these messages were received. These messages were delivered in ostensibly homogenous spaces where members of the same racial group were having an internal conversation about the state of their group. However, the homogeneity of the space was undermined by the presence of cameras that broadcasted these conversations across the globe. Dual audiences, then, reshaped the potential interpretation of the entire event.

Barack Obama as a Deracialized Candidate

Almost immediately after the 2008 election, the media began to discuss whether or not the country had entered a postracial period, the suggestion being that the election of a Black president demonstrated the ability of whites to see beyond race and simply vote for their candidate of choice (Remnick 2008; Steele 2008; Schorr 2008). Others argued that the new Black president was able to get elected without making race the major focus of his campaign (Bai 2008; Smith and Martin 2008; Serwer 2008). Obama's victory signaled a transitional moment in American history in which its history of African enslavement and racial prejudice was replaced by a period of racial openness and true adherence to the

American ideals of freedoms and equality (Steele 2008). While his Blackness portended much for racial tolerance, Obama's mixed-race heritage was also seen as symbolically important (Harwood 2008; Carroll 2008). Watching footage of Obama's family and seeing his extended family on the campaign trail presented a portrait of a multiracial family that represented the American racial mosaic (Terry 2008). He was the son of white mother and Kenyan father, the husband of a Black wife, the father of Black daughters, and the brother of an Asian sister (Niesse 2008). The visual told a story of American racial progress that was powerful for many Americans and resonated with a cross-section of voters.

Obama's campaign style was a new-millennium take on an older style among Black candidates. Black candidates understood that if they were to be elected to higher office, they had to figure out a way to diminish the negative impact of their race on their electoral ambitions. In their examination of the 1989 election that ushered in the first Black governor of Virginia, Democrat Doug Wilder, and Black mayors in New York City, Cleveland, Seattle, and several other majority-white municipalities, Joseph P. McCormick and Charles E. Jones (1993) highlight two important anomalies in this election cycle. First, these officials were elected in non-Black districts that bucked previous trends, even though many believed that whites would not vote cross-racially and particularly not for Black candidates (Reeves 1997). More important, McCormick and Jones highlighted another anomaly in these election outcomes that is particularly relevant here. They argued that these candidates engaged in a campaign strategy called deracialization, which they defined as,

> conducting a campaign in a stylistic fashion that defuses the polar-izing effects of race by avoiding explicit references to race-specific

issues, while at the same time emphasizing those issues that are perceived as *racially transcendent*, thus mobilizing a broad segment of the electorate for purposes of capturing or maintaining public office. (McCormick and Jones 1993, 76; italics added)

Simply put, these candidates avoided direct engagement with race or any racialized topic or image beyond things that were out of their control, such as phenotype. According to these scholars, deracialization impacted three areas of campaign strategy: "political style, mobilization tactics, and issues." These new deracialized candidates worked to dispel white voters' perceptions of Black candidates as angry insurgent candidates. They had to exhibit a nonthreatening demeanor while refraining from making explicit racial appeals to the Black community and avoiding issues that are or could potentially be viewed as being race-specific. These tactics provided enough distance from the Black community to make the Black candidate more palatable to white voters. Since the 1989 election, the number of Black candidates who have taken on variations of this deracialized strategy and successfully been elected to office has increased significantly.[2] Barack Obama's ascendency to the White House is the most important endorsement of this electoral strategy.

The key to the effectiveness of more recent deracialized candidates is their "story." Former White House senior political advisor David Axelrod, who specialized in consulting for Black mayoral candidates before working for the Obama campaign and administration, highlighted the importance of candidates' personal stories in an article in *The Nation* in 2007, where he suggested that the best asset of Black candidates with whom he worked was "the direct, lived experience of the effects of injustice with a simultaneous faith that the injustice wasn't permanent, that it could be overcome" (quoted in Hayes 2007).[3] Although Black candidates by virtue of phenotype offer a constant reminder of America's history of racial injustice, deracialized candidates—through the symbolism of their story and the style of their campaign—render that history part of the past and offer a hopeful view of the present.

Deracialized candidates avoid talking about race because they believe their raced bodies silently cue white voters to think about race. Adding words to that cue seems to emphasize racial differences instead of making voters more comfortable with voting for Blacks. For the most part, as a candidate, Obama focused on his story and the ways that story demonstrated racial unity rather than division. In his skillful management of race, he successfully downplayed the importance of his race in the campaign and avoided most discussions about it. However, he was able to talk about race in one particular way: he could talk about Black pathology as frequently as he wanted without much opposition.

Defining Black Blame

Citizens want to understand and explain persistent racial inequality. As Blacks and other Americans attempt to reconcile core American values with persistent unequal outcomes, it is expected that they also look to assign blame. Who is responsible? Evidence from my previous works suggests that there were two general targets for blame, either structural forces (system blame) or Blacks themselves (Black blame) (Price 2009). Blacks who see the American political system as inherently hostile to Black interests, either intentionally or through more benign forms of racial privilege, are more likely to see the American government and its agents as responsible for racial inequality—in other words to engage in *system blame*. Alternatively, some believe that contemporary inequalities can be explained by poor choices that Blacks make. In an era where Blacks have more access to the centers of power and opportunities to succeed than at any other time in American history, they see hard-earned political capital being squandered by the consistently misplaced priorities of the youth who are making poor choices. As a result, they engage in a process of *Black blame*.

The focus here is on how President Obama uses rhetoric that blames Blacks. However, neither the conceptual framework of blaming Blacks nor the strategic uses of rhetoric to do so are new developments. Inherent in most pursuits of racial uplift has been the judgment (most often on the part of middle-class Blacks) that poorer Blacks are not living up to high moral or social standards (Gaines 1996). Even Black nationalists who prioritize racial pride believe that most Blacks need to experience some kind of cognitive liberation process in which they purge themselves of internalized standards of Black inferiority (Harris-Lacewell 2006; Dawson 2001). Nationalists argue that this false consciousness drives the destructive behavior of Blacks. Black blame and system blame are not mutually exclusive processes; presumably one can believe that the government enacts policies that are hostile to Black progress *and* that Blacks make choices that hinder progress. In my research, however, most often people emphasize one or the other and the direction of emphasis has an impact on which policy preferences and prescriptions they support (Price 2009). Shortly before Obama began his campaign, a high-profile debate about this topic emerged, initiated by statements made by Bill Cosby.

"Come on, people," was both the pleading refrain Bill Cosby offered during his national Call Out tour. It is also the title of his book with Harvard physician Alvin F. Poussaint. In the tour (of mostly Black churches) and in the book, Cosby extended the narrative he initiated in 2004 at an NAACP gala to commemorate the fiftieth anniversary of *Brown v. Board of Education*, in which he called on particular segments of the Black community (e.g., the poor, single mothers, and youth) to take responsibility for their destructive life choices and the negative outcomes that resulted (Cosby and Poussaint 2007). According to Cosby (2004), "the lower economic and lower middle economic people are not holding their end in this deal." They were letting down the civil rights generation by engaging in a long list of dysfunctional behaviors such as poor parenting, making unwise financial choices, engaging in criminal acts, giving their children ethnic names, and making problematic fashion choices. For instance, at the NAACP dinner, Cosby said,

> In our cities and public schools we have 50% dropout. In our own neighborhood, we have men in prison. No longer is a person embarrassed because they're pregnant without a husband. No longer is a boy considered an embarrassment if he tries to run away from being the father of the unmarried child. (Cosby 2004)

Although Cosby was not the first African American to use tropes of personal responsibility to explain persistent community problems, his initial outburst and subsequent reaffirmation reignited this debate among African Americans.[4] Many questioned the truth of Cosby's statements, whether he had enough moral authority to be the one making them, and whether or not these things needed to be said at all. Ted Shaw, then director of the NAACP Legal and Education Defense Fund, which sponsored the event, rose immediately after Cosby spoke to offer a counterpoint to Cosby's assertions. He noted that many of the problems the Black community faced were not of its own making and were the result of discriminatory policies beyond their control (Meyer 2004).

However, Kweisi Mfume, a former congressman and the former head of the NAACP, agreed with Cosby and gave him credit for saying what needed to be said, as did many Black other commentators (Tucker 2004). According to them, Cosby had engaged in a "tough love" conversation with Black people, especially certain community members, that was long overdue.

Less than four years later, Barack Obama announced his intention to run for president and began campaigning across the country. While doing so, he made statements that can be read as Cosby-esque. However, instead of reigniting the heated debate over both the message and the appropriateness of the speaker, Obama's comments were largely unknown or unacknowledged. To some extent, Obama and Cosby occupied similar social spaces where both the strength of connection to the targets of their critique and their authority to speak to these particular community issues was fragile at best. Cosby's status as a crossover comic with a mostly white audience and Obama's status as a relative newcomer to the national Black political scene created some social distance between them and most Black people. The difference, however, was that at least with Cosby there was a debate. When the political stake of the presidency came into play, debate was largely silenced and unwelcomed.

There is no question that Barack Obama used personal responsibility tropes and characterizations of Black behavior that qualify as Black blame. Whether chiding Blacks for poor parenting, for dysfunctional priorities, or for being too apathetic, Obama made clear throughout the campaign and his presidency that there was much work to be done by Blacks themselves if community outcomes were to improve. The work that he prescribed was not only necessary but a unique set of objectives for African Americans that he did not offer to other racial groups. Instead, he made pointed statements to Blacks about the need, to quote *Chicago Sun-Times* columnist Lynn Sweet (2008), "to shape up." Obama's use of Black blame achieved two goals: he demonstrated to ordinary Black people that he was connected to them and understood their challenges, and he signaled to whites his ability to serve as an objective critic of Black behavior. He was able to do these two things simultaneously by invoking Black blame as an racial insider at predominantly Black events that before the 2008 election were essentially safe spaces for Blacks (or the producers of what Michael Dawson [2001] calls the Black counterpublic). In Black churches and at majority-Black events, he dispensed blame as if he was engaged in a conversation with a bunch of old friends who needed and didn't mind a good talking to. His rhetorical style and mannerisms took on the tone of a southern Baptist minister rather than that of a Harvard-educated law professor. He engaged the audience with call and response and other racialized cues. Simultaneously, he was speaking as a racial interlocutor who, like members of other racial groups, questioned the values and priorities of certain segments of the Black community. This "talking to" was done within earshot of non-Blacks. When they saw him telling Blacks to take responsibility for themselves, they believed that Obama understood the problems they saw as endemic and widespread among Blacks. In short, he tapped into beliefs that are the foundation of modern racial resentment (Kinder and Sanders 1996).

Obama's deployment of Black blame coupled with his deracialized campaign style and his characterization of the role of race in contemporary America presents real difficulties for Black politics. During the campaign, he asserted that racism was largely in the past and invoked Black blame to indict Blacks who pointed to continuing racism as a reason for failure within the community. When Black blame is coupled with this view of American race relations,

Blacks and their advocates are placed in the impossible position of being marginalized either as disgruntled holdovers who cannot release the past or as people who are so myopic they cannot see beyond their own narrow struggles to coalesce with like-minded people of other races. Either way, the combination creates a hostile environment for making race-specific claims related to problems that continue to plague the African American community.

Obama: In His Own Words

The speeches examined in this chapter were delivered in front of majority-Black audiences to rousing success and raucous applause. While Obama uses Black blame frequently, he never does so before non-Black audiences. I begin with Obama's Selma speech because it represents one of his earliest invocations of Black blame on the campaign trail. However, I provide examples that continue well into his second term. These examples are taken from transcripts of formal and informal speeches that were covered by the national press and broadcast to national audiences.

Selma

On March 4, 2007, veteran activists and ministers from the civil rights movement came together to commemorate the Selma marches for voting rights, a series of three marches from Montgomery to Selma, Alabama, that took place in 1965. The first of these marches was dubbed Bloody Sunday because of the ruthless violence Alabama state troopers visited upon the protesters. As the marchers attempted to cross the Edmund Pettus Bridge in Selma, they were met by a battalion of state troopers who ordered them to disband and within seconds began to brutally attack them. Many marchers were beaten bloody. Two more attempts were required before the protestors were able to successfully complete the march. During the campaign for the 2008 presidency, there was a media spotlight on the commemoration of this seminal Civil Right movement event after Obama and Hillary Clinton were both invited to participate. At this point in the campaign, which of the two candidates would receive the bulk of the Black vote was still an open question.[5] The Clintons had deep and strong ties to the Black community, especially during Bill Clinton's two administrations, and Barack Obama had only recently declared his intention to run. Ultimately, Clinton and Obama delivered dueling speeches in separate churches in Selma.

In his speech at the Brown Chapel AME Church, after recognizing various dignitaries who were in attendance, Obama began by relaying his story, as he did so often on the campaign trail. However, instead of equating his story with a universal narrative of American progress and promise, he connected it directly to the civil rights struggle. As a relatively new candidate on the campaign trail who was still being introduced to most audiences, Obama discussed the similarities between his Black immigrant father's experiences with British colonizers in Kenya and Black experiences in the Jim Crow South. In this way, he established his racial bona fides and status as a community insider. For the rest of the speech he outlined the heroic efforts of the civil rights generation and the level of indebtedness all subsequent generations had to them for those efforts. Peniel Joseph (2010, 170) suggests that "like most Americans, especially those coming of age in the aftermath of the [civil rights] movement's peak, Obama at times conflates popular memory of the era with actual history in his reminisces of the period." As a result, he draws conclusions about this period's influence on the present that resonate with audiences and obscure important historical linkages.

These heroes and their efforts, according to Obama, were not being adequately appreciated. Thus he engaged in Black blame as he discussed the ways that younger Blacks have failed to live up to the ideals of the civil rights movement. According to him, they have lost sight of the values and moral priorities previous generations exemplified. At one point he suggested that commitment of previous generations to public service and community empowerment have been replaced by greed and materialism. For Obama (2007), this new generation of Blacks "thinks it doesn't have to make as many sacrifices. . . . Thinks that the very height of ambition is to make as much money as you can, to drive the biggest car and have the biggest house, and wear a Rolex watch and get your own private jet, get some of that Oprah money." Further, he asserted that these misplaced values were not only in opposition to the values of the previous generations, but they were also morally empty without some level of commitment to service. He said,

> There's nothing wrong with making money, but if you know your history, then you know that there is a certain poverty of ambition involved in simply striving just for money. Materialism alone will not fulfill the possibilities of your existence. You have to fill that with something else. You have to fill it with the golden rule. You've got to fill it with thinking about others. And if we know our history, then we will understand that that is the highest mark of service.
>
> I can't say for certain that we have instilled that same sense of moral clarity and purpose in this generation. Bishop, sometimes I feel like we've lost it a little bit. (Obama 2007)

In subsequent paragraphs of the speech, Obama questioned a mentality among young Blacks that regards speaking proper English and reading as acting white and offered other examples of their misguided behavior.

The previous quote was a very mild form of rebuke, but later in the speech Obama's usage of Black blame took on a sharper and clearer tone. When discussing what he labeled as "complaining" about persistent inequality and the government's role in fomenting inequality, he acknowledged that the government had a role but added,

> We understand [there are problems in the government], but I'll tell you what. I also know that if *cousin Pookie* would vote, get off the couch and register some folks and go to the polls, we might have a different kind of politics. . . . Take off your bedroom slippers. Put on your marching shoes. (Obama 2007; italics added)

This statement received significant applause. Little was said about the fact that he was suggesting that government failure to address problems of inequality was the result of political apathy in the Black community. It is important to note that implicit in his assertion was a class critique as well. Presumably, Obama and middle-class Blacks are not this "cousin Pookie" he spoke of, nor are they the ones wearing the bedroom slippers. Thus, this rebuke of the other was a reprimand to poor Blacks for their destructive behavior. He went further when discussing the fact that so many Black children live in poverty. He started by suggesting that this was a problem everybody should ashamed of, then added, "But don't tell me it doesn't have a little to do with the fact that we got too many daddies not acting like daddies" (Obama 2007). In this speech, Obama was channeling Cosby's arguments—with one exception. Obama attributed some blame to structural and governmental inequality; in his view, however, any fault of the government paled in comparison to internal community problems.

Father's Day Speech

On Father's Day 2008, Obama celebrated at Apostolic Church of God on Chicago's predominantly Black South Side. Unlike the Selma speech, which commemorated a particular moment in American racial history, there was no reason to offer any race-specific commentary at this event. It could have just as easily been an opportunity to present himself as a positive family man and attentive father: he had just become the presumptive presidential nominee and his campaign was stockpiling money. Yet he delivered a speech about the absence and failures of fathers in the Black community. Before offering Black blame, he outlined the pervasive problems that plague the Black community—truancy, crime, and failing schools, among other problems. The plight of Black children was of deep concern to Obama and the congregation, and on Father's Day it was the absence of men that was being examined. As in Selma, he acknowledged that there was a role for government to play in addressing these issues, but ultimately African Americans needed to take collective and individual responsibility for their children. "But [Black people] also need families to raise our children. We need fathers to realize that responsibility does not end at conception. We need them to realize that what makes you a man is not the ability to have a child—it's the courage to raise one" (Obama 2008c). He even dressed down fathers who were present in this speech; he chided fathers who hadn't physically abandoned their families for not setting better examples for their children. Instead of being engaged and active participants in the lives of their children, they had emotionally checked out. He lectured,

It's a wonderful thing if you are *married and living* in a home with your children, but don't just sit in the house and watch "SportsCenter" all weekend long. That's why so many children are growing up in front of the television. As fathers and parents, we've got to spend more time with them, and help them with their homework, and replace the video game or the remote control with a book once in a while. That's how we build that foundation. (Obama 2008c; my italics)

He spoke as one Black father speaking to other Black fathers. In this speech, he inserted his story in the middle of his address when he talked about single mothers who are left behind to care for their children alone.

He recounted the stories of how his mother, with the help of his grandparents, raised him without his father. The condition of single motherhood and the image of the longsuffering single mother who sacrifices for her children are iconic in the African American community. He played on this popular image while telling his story. His fleshing out of his use of the image illustrates how he sometimes muddled or manipulated racial rhetoric. He focused on the struggles of his mother and other single mothers, but he was comparing two distinct racial images. The Black single mother in the mind of most is a woman with low skills, low pay, and minimal education. His mother, however, was a well-educated white academic. Though the challenges these women face may be similar, the realities of their experiences are quite different. Even he admitted that this childhood was not as "tough as many young people today" (Obama 2008c). However, his conflation of the two has the effects of grounding him in a particular Black experience he did not have, reaffirming his insider credentials, and further legitimizing his use of Black blame.

Texas Stump Speech

Thus far Obama's uses of Black blame have been fairly moderate. If it were not for the settings and the reference to "Pookie," these narratives would hardly have taken on obvious racial overtones. Without the racial specificity, Obama merely offered prescriptions for good living that could garner widespread support among members of any group. But he was direct about the fact that he was speaking to unique concerns within his own community—the African American community. An example of a more stringent form of Black blame came from accounts of a less formal stump speech Obama made while trying to win the Texas Democratic primary. He gave this speech before a mostly Black crowd in the small east Texas city of Beaumont. His criticism was more severe not because of his direct invocation of race but because his characterization of Black parenting resonates with popular negative stereotypes of Blacks. His comment that he was aware that some people might be offended provides some evidence that he understood that he was treading a fine line.

In this speech, Obama reiterated the need for parents to model the behavior that they wanted to see in their children. In this particular speech, he accomplished this by instructing parents about the kinds of things they needed to do to increase the educational achievement for Black children. He began,

> Turn off the TV set, put the video game away. Buy a little desk or put that child by the kitchen table. Watch them do their homework. If they don't know how to do it, give them help. If you don't know how to do it, call the teacher. Make them go to bed at a reasonable time. Keep them off the streets. Give 'em some breakfast. Come on. . . . You know I am right. (quoted in BET Staff 2008)

It is very difficult for any parent or interested observer—Black or white—to disagree. His prescription was one that makes for a successful student and healthy childhood. However, as he continued this speech and offered more advice, his frame became less universal, more racially laden, and his characterization of the people he was talking about clearly pathological. Obama continued,

> I know how hard it is to get kids to eat properly. But I also know that if folks letting our children drink eight sodas a day, which some parents do, or, you know, eat a bag of potato chips for lunch, or Popeyes for breakfast. Y'all have Popeyes out in Beaumont? I know some of y'all you got that cold Popeyes out for breakfast. I know. That's why y'all laughing . . . You can't do that. Children have to have proper nutrition. That affects also how they study, how they learn in school. (quoted in BET Staff 2008)

A reporter from the *Chicago Sun-Times* noted that these statements received "raucous applause from the mostly Black audience" (Sweet 2008). The reference to fried chicken alone should give one pause, but Obama seemed to have tapped into African American frustrations. As the racial collective (of which Obama is a part) searched for remedies, members within the group were faulted or blamed. Not just any Black was blamed, however. The people in the audience were applauding, so they probably did not see themselves as culprits. No, the worst offenders were those elusive others who failed to show up to political events and Father's Day events. Their choices marked the entire race.

Obama's Racial Vision

To understand the message imparted by Obama's use of Black blame, one must put them in the context of his larger view of race relations in America. I argued earlier that in the 2008 election the impact of Black blame, as a conceptual and political tool, cannot be understood unless we also examine Obama's campaign strategies that kept racial politics at the margins and relied on more universal narratives. Interestingly, we did not learn very much about Obama's views on race because they were intentionally muted. He understood that this campaign was historic and had special meaning for Blacks. He initiated a discussion about race only once, when he was in the throes of the Jeremiah Wright controversy and seemed to have no other choice. Chapter 3 is devoted to this speech, but it is important to briefly discuss here the ways it invoked Black blame.

Interestingly, he also equated the possibility of completely shunning Rev. Wright with abandoning his racial identity or rejecting white members of his own family who harbored racial prejudices. For him, all of these choices were less than optimal because of the depth of connection he had to these people. Wright's controversial statements posed two dilemmas for Obama. First, he had to distance himself from what was being portrayed as anti-Americanism on the part of his pastor of twenty years. Second, he had to do this without alienating African Americans for whom the Black church serves as a pivotal religious and social institution. African Americans were excited about the prospect of a Black president, but the Black church continues to hold a special place in the minds of many Blacks. They continue to see their churches not only as religious institutions but also as social service agencies and sources of political knowledge (McDaniel 2008; Harris 1999; Calhoun-Brown

1996). Therefore, even if Blacks saw the need to jettison Wright, Obama still needed to tread carefully. By all accounts he successfully navigated this dilemma and received widespread praise for his "A More Perfect Union" speech.

Toward the end of the speech, President Obama proposed a way forward by addressing Blacks and whites separately. African Americans needed to build coalitions with whites and other racial groups in order to achieve bigger goals, he said. However, these coalitions would be viable only if African Americans did not become "victims of their past." For Obama, the way forward was to connect to broad policies that appeal to "the larger aspirations of all Americans." Notably, he ended this direct appeal with a personal responsibility trope.

> And it means taking full responsibility for our own lives—by demanding more from our fathers, and spending more time with our children, and reading to them, and teaching them that while they may face challenges and discrimination in their own lives, they must never succumb to despair or cynicism; they must always believe that they can write their own destiny. (Obama 2008b)

This particular iteration of the personal responsibility refrain resonates with all the other speeches examined in this chapter. The fact that he made a special plea to Blacks suggests that he believed that many Blacks were not in fact "taking full responsibility for their lives" and that they were "succumbing to despair or cynicism."

After addressing Blacks, he addressed whites and urged them to see "that what ails the African American community does not just exist in the minds of Black people." He implored them to support government efforts to ensure fairness and justice for all Americans through the enforcement of civil right laws and investment in public education. The actions he identified are really prescriptions for government action. Nowhere did he make individualized suggestions for whites to "take full responsibility" for their personal prejudices or microaggressions toward Blacks. Only Blacks warrant a special note about personal responsibility and self-reliance in Obama's speech.

Black Blame from the White House

Much of what has been shared so far came from candidate Obama. However, President Obama offered similar condemnations. Two notable moments highlighted here are his Morehouse College commencement speech and his speech commemorating the fiftieth anniversary of the March on Washington. Both speeches were given during the summer of 2013 and in front of majority-Black audiences. These speeches were moments when President Obama was free to talk about his connection to the African American community and the place of that community in American society. The commencement and the commemoration were also times for reflection on Black progress and discussions of hope for the future. Obama offered numerous congratulatory remarks, but those remarks were tempered by remonstrations. Interestingly, Obama prefaced his chastisement in both speeches with the same statement: "if *we're* honest with *ourselves.*" It is clear that he was talking as a member of the Black community engaging in straight talk with other members. Colloquially, he was engaged in real talk. This raises problematic questions about audience that will be addressed later in the chapter. For now, I turn to the speeches.

Obama offered a rhetorical one-two punch of flattering and shaming in one particularly long passage during his commencement address at Morehouse. His words were particularly stinging because they were being made at the prestigious historically Black men's college that has produced some of Black America's most important male leaders, academics, and entertainers. Hence, when he offered his critique it was during a moment of celebration of these young men's success. These were kids who had done the right thing by going to college and finishing their degrees. In that particular moment, they had beaten the odds, defied the statistics, risen above the challenges that young Black men face in this country. These achievements were met by Obama's "honesty." He offered, "But that doesn't mean we don't have work—*because if we're honest with ourselves*, we know that too few of our brothers have the opportunities that you've had here at Morehouse" (Obama 2013a; italics added). In a context in which barely a quarter of African American men graduate from college, Obama pointed to the amazing opportunity that these men had shared with each other and that set them apart from many in their community. However, this celebration was short-lived as Obama turned to the shortcomings of Black men who were not at Morehouse who lacked personal responsibility. He used his own experiences to highlight the problem.

> We know that too many young men in our community continue to make bad choices. And I have to say, growing up, I made quite a few myself. Sometimes I wrote off my own failings as just another example of the world trying to keep a black man down. I had a tendency sometimes to make excuses for me not doing the right thing. But one of the things that all of you have learned over the last four years is there's no longer any room for excuses. (Obama 2013a)

As Obama spoke to these young men and their families on one of the most important days of their lives, he used the moment to admonish the Black community for its failures. He told this graduating class that they shouldn't make excuses, even in the face of actual discrimination, which he openly acknowledged the existence of. Obama affirmed the continued presence of racial discrimination in America. He told them that excuses would not work and that it was "not because the bitter legacy of slavery and segregation have vanished entirely; they have not. Not because racism and discrimination no longer exist; we know those are still out there" (Obama 2013a). Despite the reality that systemic hurdles create hierarchies that do not reward individual merit, according to Obama, these young men needed to understand that individual merit is the *only* answer because "nobody is going to give you anything that you have not earned." Moreover, Obama assured them, "Nobody cares how tough your upbringing was. Nobody cares if you suffered some discrimination" (Obama 2013a). The biggest problem with this statement is that his job is literally to care about these things and their impact on all Americans, including Blacks.

The highest-ranking Black politician and political official of any type in the world points to the paradox of race relations in America—that even though racism is fertile and widespread, African Americans are still supposed to use principles related to equality and meritocracy put forth by the dominant group to govern their behavior. He does not talk about ways that such a system can be dismantled, he does not point to strategies previous generations have used, *and* he does not point to ways he can bring his power to bear on the problem. In fact, he uses the struggles of African American foremothers and forefathers not as models of resistance and resilience to prevailing racial orders but as examples of people who didn't rely on excuses. This rhetoric obscures African American history by suggesting that previous generations simply put their heads down and silently suffered. It erases the work they did to create counternarratives and parallel institutions to meet the needs of the community while simultaneously pushing for social change.

His presence at the commencement, as with everything the president does, was widely reported and there was some discussion of his statements and their appropriateness. Debates erupted on social media about Obama's comments. The difficulty seemed to lie in whether the comments were appropriate for the occasion and whether they were a sign that Obama was out of touch (Coates 2013; Eilperin 2013).[6] A discussion also emerged about the particular way that Obama addressed Black audiences in venues that went beyond this one event. Most critics wanted to know why these "tough love" conversations were reserved for the community that has offered him the most consistent support without asking very much of him. The fact that there was public debate about these comments makes this a unique moment. More remarkable, and likely a compounding factor in sparking debate, Michelle Obama (2013) weighed in on the subject. While giving the commencement at another historically Black college, Bowie State in Maryland, Mrs. Obama echoed her husband's suggestion that Black youth were somehow betraying the struggles of their ancestors. Using similar imagery, she told the audience,

> But today, more than 150 years after the Emancipation Proclamation, more than 50 years after the end of "separate but equal," when it comes to getting an education, too many of our young people just can't be bothered. Today, instead of walking miles every day to school, they're sitting on couches for hours playing video games, watching TV. Instead of dreaming of being a teacher or a lawyer or a business leader, they're fantasizing about being a baller or a rapper.

Although there was no reason to believe that the Obamas had divergent perspectives, prior to this speech Mrs. Obama had been silent or her words were not reported. At Bowie State she made clear that she agreed with his "often" used comments: "And as my husband has said often, please stand up and reject the slander that says a black child with a book is trying to act white. Reject that" (M. Obama 2013). After this commencement, there was no doubt that both Obamas were invested in a narrative of Black pathology as the source of stalled Black progress. There is no way to glean whether her analysis was tied to more structural arguments that might balance her use of personal responsibility tropes. What is known is that like her husband, she chose to give these comments to a largely Black audience. Her comment about books is particularly troubling, given that she was speaking at a college, where it would seem that reading books was de rigueur.

Just a few months later, at the commemoration of fiftieth anniversary of the 1963 March on Washington, the president gave remarks about the significance of the march. As he had done in many of his other speeches, Obama pointed to the sharp schism between the goals of the civil rights movement and the current behavior of some African Americans, though how many was quite vague.

> *If we're honest with ourselves*, we'll admit that during the course of 50 years, there were times when some of us claiming to push for change lost our way. The anguish of assassinations set off self-defeating riots. Legitimate grievances against police brutality tipped into excuse-making for criminal behavior. (Obama 2013b; italics added)

Obama further elaborated on the challenges African Americans face and how they should respond, using a signature rhetorical move in which he talked about the fact that racial politics require the efforts of all groups while addressing what Blacks ought to be doing to make race relations better.

> Racial politics could cut both ways, as the transformative message of unity and brotherhood was drowned out by the language of re-crimination. And what had once been a call for equality of opportunity, the chance for all Americans to work hard and get ahead was too often framed as a mere desire for government support—as if we had no agency in our own liberation, as if poverty was an excuse for not raising your child, and the bigotry of others was reason to give up on yourself. (Obama 2013b)

The March on Washington signified powerful resistance and a push toward greater liberation for African American people during one of the most significant social movements in American history. Fifty years later, the effects of the civil rights movement mark every area of American life. There is virtually no space where its impact is not felt, yet President Obama used this historic anniversary to once again highlight the ways Black people had failed. His reliance on Black blame transformed quite smoothly from campaign rhetoric to governing rhetoric. It is important to understand the potential impact of this seamless transformation because governing rhetoric is often the basis for real policies and legislative initiatives.

Obama and His Audience(s)

Although the content of Obama's statements upbraiding Blacks for what he sees as problematic behavior is important, an equally important discussion emerges about the importance of audience and the disintegration of safe spaces in the Black community. His characterization (or mischaracterization) of the motives and behavioral tendencies of Blacks all happen in places that have not been hidden from white gaze but have certainly been less accessible to them because they exist in the Black public sphere—Black colleges, Black churches, Black radio programs, and Black newspapers. A lot of work has been done on the role of the Black public sphere in Black decision making and opinion formation. However, Obama's election has opened that sphere to larger scrutiny and leaving its participants vulnerable to Obama's problematic critique and from non-Blacks. I now turn to the role of audiences in shaping the context in which Obama's words are consumed by both Black and non-Black audiences.

Though the words Obama uses can tell us an enormous amount about his perspective on race and racial issues, this argument is about more than his words or even the impact of the words. It is about the use of particular narratives in conjunction with particular optics and in front of particular audiences. Part of the reason why Obama was able to say many of these things is because he is a Black president saying them in front of Black audiences who want to both preserve and protect this important historical moment. The paradox of this desire is that once these speeches are broadcast beyond the walls of whatever Black church or historically Black college or university Obama is visiting, the meaning moves beyond a "tough love" conversation to become an excoriation of Blacks. At this point, it can be read as the president laying out his problems with the Black community to a white audience, a stance that many Blacks would find much more egregious. This expanded audience and altered meaning shifts the discussion to a common narrative in the larger society that claims that Blacks simply do not try hard enough. It taps into notions of racial resentment that are predicated on the belief that Blacks are not able to get ahead because they fail to adhere to the American creed and work ethic (Kinder and Sanders 1996). This change simultaneously precludes discussion about institutionalized racism and other structural barriers to success because the frame Obama employs is confined to individual effort or lack thereof.

It is also very clear that Barack Obama understands the nature of the space he occupies when he makes such speeches and that the context is very different from other campaign stops. Thus far, we've discussed the race-specific content Obama used in his interactions with Blacks, but the performative style he used for Black audiences also became race-specific. His body language and cadence shifted in ways that signaled his ease in his community of origin. His style was more that of a minister than that of conventional politician. In an interview with National Public Radio (NPR) leading up to the Selma commemoration, a reporter asked Obama about the difference in the way he talked to Black and white audiences. Obama responded:

> I think that the themes are consistent. It think that there's a certain black idiom that it's hard not to slip into when you're talking to a black audience because of the audience response. It's the classic call and response. Anybody who's spent time in a black church knows what I mean. And so you get a little looser; it becomes a little more like jazz and a little less like a set score. (quoted in Inskeep 2007)

That Obama adjusted his style for particular audiences is not surprising. He understands racial differences in communication and points to concepts like call and response and musical genres like jazz that specifically resonate with and reference Blackness. The ability to pay attention to the mood and expectations of an audience accounts for why some public speakers are so much better than others. It is certainly pivotal to the success of a race whisperer.

Changing linguistic forms from Standard English to more colloquial English, commonly referred to as code switching, is a common practice for many Blacks.[7] That individuals speak differently in the company of intimates and other members of their identity groups is expected, as is speaking more formally in more public spaces. The problem these public addresses present is that Obama spoke as if he was only among members of his identity group, but he was not. He was on the national, even the international, stage. The gravity of what was happening was obscured by the visibility of the racial composition of the room and the invisibility of the larger, more heterogeneous viewing audience. Without careful attention, it was easy to miss this dynamic of the dual audience and how the message was received by multiple listeners. He was airing the Black community's dirty laundry in public, which is not generally seen as a good thing. Obama, however, was given a pass for this transgression.

It should be stated at the outset that for all the speeches discussed in this chapter many African Americans in the audience agreed with his assessments. That agreement was clearly expressed through applause and cheering. Although the audience in the room where the speeches were delivered was overwhelmingly Black, all of these speeches received major news coverage and the formal speeches were broadcast live on cable news and in many cases were rebroadcast on C-SPAN. In all of the coverage, there was almost no critique of his rebukes of African Americans; if they were mentioned at all it was mostly referred to as "tough love" conversations. There was virtually no suggestion that people in the room disapproved of the message he offered. No instances of audience protests were reported, and available video footage does not suggest any disagreement from the audience. Coverage tended to focus on the more universal aspects of the speeches, such as his positions on education or other policy matters.

We have no way of quantifying who in these spaces may have disagreed with his assertions. We do know that who is listening impacts what we say, and who can hear what is being said impacts the speaker and the listener (Banjo 2013). Obama's narrative of Black pathology is potentially perceived differently by Black and non-Black audiences. These perceptions then result in widely varying political preferences and policy prescriptions. However, audience and its role in this discussion serves as an invisible but powerful influence in understanding the impact of Obama's reliance on Black pathology narratives. The fact that they are reserved for majority or exclusively Black audiences produces two important results. First, no matter how he phrases his rhetoric, the visual image is always of Black people applauding and responding positively to his presentation. Without knowing the words, the visual presentation of his interaction with the audience is that of complete support or approval. Thus, his excoriation of Blacks, at least on the surface, is done with the resounding approval of his Black audience. Second, the fact that he reserves this trope exclusively for Black audiences suggests that the intent is to convey the idea that only Blacks merit this kind of "tough love." There can be little doubt that he is making a connection specifically for Blacks who need and deserve the moral lessons he provides. Obama asserts very clearly the idea that he communicates with Black audiences in a special way. Because this narrative is specifically and continually repeated to Blacks only, the only conclusion that can be drawn is that Obama sees this as a Black problem.

Political rhetoric does not always result in clear policy goals. Alternatively, policy goals and preferences are not always preceded by strong attempts at persuasion through rhetoric. However, when politicians speak, whether their rhetoric has substantive aims or not, their words are always symbolically important. Obama's decision to make these statements, where he chooses to make them, and the narrow audiences he reserves them for pose difficult challenges to the way we currently understand political debate. First, real questions emerge regarding the continued existence of Black safe spaces in which Blacks can hash out community issues and develop some semblance of a Black agenda. Significant scholarship has focused on the role of the Black public sphere in the transmission of intraracial beliefs and ideas. When Obama visits these spaces, it is not just as a politician gaining temporary access to a Black church or fraternal group but as a member of a racial group whose membership gives him complete access. The difficulty lies in the fact that he is also showing up, first, as a high-profile political figure and, eventually, as leader of the free world. With that comes a different level of scrutiny in these spaces because mainstream political actors, pundits, and media outlets all get to observe and weigh in on what would normally be intraracial interactions. The second challenge results directly from this new scrutiny, and that is the challenge of multiple audiences and the problems stemming from multiple translations. Besides sports and a few crime procedurals, Black and white audiences don't even watch the same television shows, which suggest that they are not even necessarily getting the same cultural inputs (Nielsen Company 2011). Thus, it also comes as no surprise that these different audiences might view these statements by Obama quite differently.

Throughout history, Blacks have developed parallel institutions capable of providing services and meeting community needs that governmental and other public institutions refused to perform. Black institutions have also served as physical spaces for hosting open forums where important questions are debated. These spaces, collectively known as the Black public sphere, include churches and community centers, but in the digital world they have also come to include Black radio and television stations as well as blog sites and other Internet sources. Catherine Squires (2002, 448) describes the Black public sphere as "a set of physical or mediated spaces where people can gather and share information, debate opinions, and tease out their political interests and social needs with other participants." This is where Blacks make collective decisions about local and national demands and attempt to formulate a set of policy prescriptions that might result in collective advancement.[8] Squires also notes that the Black public sphere functions as a space for creating a "hidden transcript" used solely for and produced by community members to generate a counternarrative that challenges prevailing stereotypes, or "protest rhetoric," and for developing an independent starting point for engaging with "other publics." Prominent examples of these spaces include Black religious institutions and networks as well as historically Black colleges and universities (HBCUs). These examples in particular were the driving institutional forces behind one of the most important political movements—the civil rights movement. These spaces provided personnel and served as staging grounds and incubators for the most identifiable rhetoric about democracy and freedom in the modern era. They continue to be important forums for political discussions and information gathering (McAdam 1999; Morris 1984).

One consistency in the speeches analyzed here is that they all took place in spaces that have historically constituted the Black public sphere. They have been made at Black churches during Sunday services, at graduations at HBCUs, during gatherings at community parks, and even at civil rights commemorations. Obama is doing what community members do within these spaces: he is diagnosing problems and offering potential solutions. However, his communications travel farther and louder than those of other leaders within the sphere. Additionally, this sphere was never meant to accommodate the person who speaks for the entire country. As the physical and discursive space of a marginalized group, it is inherently a space of resistance controlled exclusively by people who are outside the mainstream. That is the opposite of the position for which candidate Barack Obama was vying. In his desire and the desire of the entire Black community to see this historical moment realized, the nature and composition of the Black public sphere was compromised.

His Selma speech illustrates the challenges well. Barack Obama, a long-shot presidential candidate, entered a Black church to commemorate one of the most important marches of the civil rights movement. His presence personified, in many ways, the success of the movement, and the congregation received him as one of their own. He provided a powerful discourse on the movement's legacy and the gratitude the nation feels for the sacrifice of movement participants. Everyone in the room was engaged in and positively responding to the themes he covered, even the pathology tropes. A wider lens, however, adds more layers to this view. An army of reporters from various media outlets was transmitting this speech to American households indiscriminately. The injection of mainstream media outlets into the physical and cognitive Black public space changed the nature of the speech. From Selma forward, this scene would be repeated and would ultimately come to a head in Obama's own church.

Interestingly, many African Americans who were in the room and were viewing from home continued to treat these moments as if nothing had changed about them. They responded as if CNN cameras were no different than the media ministry that recorded sermons every Sunday or the local Black newspaper. In fact, what was happening was qualitatively and substantively different. Instead of deacons and ushers offering commentary on the words from the pulpit, now Bill O'Reilly, Wolf Blitzer, and Chris Matthews used their national nightly shows to parse the meanings of Obama's words. In these moments, the Black public sphere lost any claims of racial insularity and intraracial collective struggle. When Obama enters Black churches and colleges, he is removing the boundaries of the Black public sphere and making ongoing discussions and debates more visible but not necessarily more legible to non-Black viewers. As soon as Obama exits, the spotlight often moves with him. There are times, with Rev. Wright for instance, where Obama's presence makes these institutions more vulnerable to mainstream examination by people who lack knowledge of social and historical contexts or cultural empathy. Ultimately, what gets reported is not robust debate about individual responsibility versus institutionalized discrimination. Instead, there are accounts of Barack Obama's nod toward the need for more personal responsibility in the Black community and a visual image of resounding Black support via applause and standing ovations. This narrow presentation provides snapshots of Obama's view of Black America, but not the totality of the views of the community.

The genius of Obama presenting pathology narratives in Black spaces is that we see Blacks supporting his assertions. While there is no doubt that many Blacks agree with Obama's views, the comfort level Blacks might feel when discussing these issues in racially heterogeneous spaces is an altogether different issue. For example, Omotayo Banjo (2013) studied the effects of watching movies containing Black stereotypes in all-Black and mixed-race audiences on African American participants. Banjo found that being in a mixed-race audience didn't influence enjoyment levels or perceptions of bias for Blacks. However, when viewing films with whites Blacks expressed "heightened" concern about whites' reactions to viewing stereotypical portrayals because of the belief that whites would be negatively influenced and less likely to interact with Blacks. Though watching a presidential candidate talking about Black issues is not exactly the same as watching a movie, Banjo's study provides some context of audience effects.

What is insidious about trumpeting Black pathology as the justification for racial inequality in widely broadcasted speeches in front of predominantly Black audiences is that the presence of whites (all non-Blacks, really) is immediate but is not clear. This makes the people who are attending the event less attentive to the impact of these kinds of statements on the multiracial interactions that are necessary in a diverse democracy. This process muddies the discursive waters, leaving only Barack Obama with clean hands. He is able to simultaneous engage in rituals of authenticity and demonstrate a form of racial objectivity.

Both the words of Obama's Black pathology narratives and the contexts in which they were spoken result in increased support from diverse communities. However, it was achieved at the expense of increased stereotyping of Blacks and an incomplete explanation of the nature of racial inequality. Although some Blacks may be focusing on the love component of these "tough love" conversations, there is no evidence to suggest that other groups are

doing the same. Indeed, Obama provides the rhetorical ammunition for decreased support for important governmental policies
that are critical to sustained efforts at reducing inequality. This
creates a difficult, if not hostile, political environment for racial
justice advocates.

2

Barack Obama, Patton's Army, and Patriotic Whiteness

I like to say that I got my name from my father, but I got
my accent—and my values—from my mother.
—Barack Obama, remarks in Osawatomie, Kansas

The choices political figures make when conveying their personal
history tells the audience a great deal about which identities they prioritize for themselves and which identities they believe will resonate
most with that audience. Their public personae are finely tailored,
and their personal histories are parsed for moments that evoke emotions and memories that ultimately lead to support at the voting
booth. Candidates seek to engage specific audiences as much as they
seek to distinguish themselves from other candidates. The previous
chapter examined the double duty that Black pathology narratives
serve. Obama's repeated invocation of Black pathology serves a dual
purpose of establishing his authenticity as a member of the Black
community and establishing himself as an objective observer who
successfully attracts both whites and Blacks to his message. In this
chapter, I turn to part of President Obama's personal history that
prioritizes a different part of his identity—his connection and proximity to whiteness. He does more than invoke a general connection to
whiteness through his maternal heritage; he connects his identity to
a particular experience of whiteness that is revered in American culture. Barack Obama's grandparents, Stanley and Madelyn Dunham,
are familial stand-ins for the prototypical World War II family whose
members did what was right for the country and then took advantage

of the policies and programs that were developed to repay them for their service. This is a generation whom the nation holds in the highest regard, and its members are the last American veterans to be held in such high regard unconditionally. While veterans since that time have returned home to much more qualified support and sometimes even hostility, veterans such as Obama's grandfather were lauded with ticker-tape parades and were the recipients of one of the largest wealth redistribution programs in American history, the GI Bill (Katznelson 2006).

Though he is widely perceived as and clearly perceives himself as African American, Obama also has a clear connection to whiteness through his maternal heritage.[1] Through Obama's own writing and many discussions about his biracial heritage, we know that President Obama spent significant portions of his life living under the care of his grandparents, and he has often discussed and written about the myriad ways they shaped his childhood and his view of the world as an adult. He was immensely proud of them and the life they made for themselves, their daughter, and her children. This was evident every time he spoke about them, as he did often on the campaign trail. Invoking these memories during the campaign also served a larger goal of mobilizing supporters and attracting votes. Because of this, it is important to discuss what Obama said about his grandparents and the process by which his grandparent's narrative emerged in his political speeches.

This chapter takes up the question of how Barack Obama invokes his connections to whiteness and to what end. One way he does this is through the invocation of his grandparents' personal experiences in World War II, which relies on a well-known iconography that is inextricably linked to whites. His narrative harkens back to what journalist Tom Brokaw (2004) calls "our greatest generation," and the imagery and the experiences he highlights often emphasize courageous sacrifice in terms of lives lost and enormous benefit for returning soldiers. The counternarrative to this characterization of the World War II generation is the story of the experiences of Blacks who suffered systematic discrimination in the military and were excluded from most postwar benefits provided to veterans. Veterans' benefits paved the way for many soldiers to become a part of the American middle class through subsidized education and home loans through federal programs that were also almost exclusively reserved for whites (Katznelson 2006; Williams 2004). Obama's decision to focus solely on the greatest generation narrative precludes acknowledgement of the opposing narrative, and it positions him as an heir to a legacy that is almost exclusively earmarked for and resonates most directly with white patriotism.

Clearly, Obama is invoking nostalgia for an earlier age when the dividing line between friends and enemies was clearer. However, given the racial hostilities that have defined American history, any nod to the past must be interrogated for larger implications, especially if we want to apply the values and norms being invoked to contemporary questions. Barack Obama is making an explicit connection to whiteness that places him in a patriotic historical tradition that elides the presence of most Blacks. Although Black veterans and their families were equally proud of their service during World War II, both the service that Blacks in the military were able to provide and the benefits after the war that were available to them were limited by discrimination. I begin with the story that Obama often shares and juxtapose it with the historical realities for African Americans during the World War II era. I then offer some arguments about what nearer proximity to whiteness achieves for President Obama.

Obama's mention of his grandparents and their connection to a particular historical moment can be easily viewed as a simple story about a candidate's family. For many who hear it, this story does not move beyond this surface level, but politicians understand the power of these kinds of stories to motivate voters to think, feel, and act in a certain way. Barack Obama adeptly uses the Dunhams to highlight an important patriotic moment that all Americans revere. The frame he uses, however, clearly becomes a racial one when he highlights iconography and political policies that are racially exclusive. If he had simply said to these audiences, "I have a white family and that gives me access to whiteness," his support among both whites and Blacks likely would have diminished. Instead, he told a story that is enveloped in racial meaning while steering clear of obvious racial conflict. He did not alienate people who prefer not to have conversations about race and he did not offend supporters who might disagree with his racial positions.

The retelling of history in political campaigns is not value free and, in fact, serves multiple purposes. First, using historical events reminds people of bygone eras and memories imprinted in our "common" national experience. Certain historical moments have been memorialized over and over again, and referencing these moments evokes important emotional responses related to patriotism and love of country. Historical memories also help voters make sense of contemporary questions. Barry Schwartz (1996, 910) argues that "collective memory" is a "model of society" and a "model for society." He explains that it consists of "reflections of [society's] needs, problems, fears, mentality and aspirations," and "defines [society's] experience, articulates its values and goals, and provides cognitive, affective, and moral orientations for realizing them." So when politicians attempt to tap into our national collective memory, they are attempting to use the historical moment as a heuristic for understanding a more complicated issue or as a vehicle for understanding contemporary questions.

The difficulty is that the relationship of the African American community to American collective memory is fraught and contentious as often as it is patriotic and joyful. While many African Americans have volunteered and served in the military since the founding of the nation, their return on this investment in nation building has often been meager or completely absent. Obama's frequent references to "Patton's army" are particularly stinging because Patton was an open and outspoken racist who questioned the role of minorities in military operations (Axelrod 2006). In addition, Black participation in the most celebrated moments of World War II was limited because "the majority of African Americans worked in the Service of Supply regiments" (Wynn 2010, 53). Thus, comparatively few of the troops who took part in D-Day landings were Black.

Using his white grandparents' story, President Obama trades on a popular narrative of national unity surrounding World War II remembrances that run counter to the experiences of most African Americans. At best, Obama's rhetoric blurs the historical narrative by discounting the struggles of African Americans during the war in favor of what Robert K. Chester (2013) calls "retroactive multiculturalism." At worst, it is an intentional obfuscation of the historical record in order to emphasize his connection to patriotic whiteness at the expense of a more complicated and racially sensitive narrative.

Barack Obama, the Dunhams, and World War II

In the 2008 and 2012 presidential campaigns, Barack Obama crisscrossed the country, sharing his message about his future plans (in 2008) and his achievements during his first term (in 2012). He talked about the economy, the ongoing U.S. wars, the limits of his opponents' visions, and many other issues, but in many of his campaign speeches he also mentioned a particular aspect of his own family history—that his grandfather fought in Patton's army and his grandmother was a "real-life Rosie the Riveter." In these conversations with potential voters and donors, President Obama was connecting himself through his grandparents to important historical images from World War II. His grandfather fought under one of the most famous and revered generals in American history, and his grandmother, like many American women doing their part for the war effort, went to work in a weapons factory. By 2012, Barack Obama's family history and his invocation of it had become commonplace. He was adept at weaving his family story into the fabric of American history, a story that tapped in to values that many white Americans shared.

The political landscape in which President Obama campaigned for the White House in 2007 was in some ways similar to the World War II era. America was trying to find its way out of a devastating downturn that impacted every part of the economy, and the nation was engaged in wars on an increasing number of fronts. The difference, however, is that we view those who came of age during the World War II era as the greatest generation in American history, and Americans today are more cynical about future possibilities than ever before. So when Obama summons the memory of his grandparents' service and sacrifice in World War II, the meaning of those memories may be open to interpretation.

Barack Obama's maternal grandfather, Stanley Dunham, a white Kansas native, enlisted in the United States Army in 1942, leaving behind a young wife, Madelyn, who was carrying their daughter, Stanley Ann. According to Dunham, he was moved to enlist after the Pearl Harbor attack that took the lives of many American soldiers and temporarily hobbled America's ability to protect itself in the Pacific theater. A few months after the attack, Stanley enlisted at Fort Leavenworth, Kansas, where he was assigned to the 1830th Ordinance Supply and Maintenance Company, Aviation, which served in the European theater of operations. His unit prepared for the invasion of France led by General George S. Patton and crossed the English Channel six weeks after Dunham enlisted (Benac 2009). Veterans who served with him remembered his dedication, his generosity, and the parties he planned while stationed in Europe. Dunham served in Europe, Asia, and North Africa. His wife did her part for the war effort by working the night shift in a plant that built B-29 bombers and taking care of their daughter during the day. Obama has often talked about the benefits of his grandfather's service, particularly the GI Bill, and how that changed the trajectory of the Dunham family's life. That government policy enabled his grandfather to attend college and his grandparents to buy a house using Veterans Administration (VA) housing loans.

Whiteness and World War II

Stanley Dunham's story is not atypical. For many young men of his generation, service in World War II was part of the experience of coming of age in the early 1940s. Young men his age were venerated for the sacrifice they made to stop Hitler's trek across Europe. They fought back against genocide and fascism and saved the world, literally. Many women served valiantly in military auxiliaries. At home, women, who were not already in the work force went to work to keep the American war machine running. All of them were viewed as patriots who embodied America's core beliefs in freedom, justice, and equality. Three-quarters of a century later, these efforts continue to inspire the awe and admiration of their descendants and the nation. David Roediger (2005) has demonstrated how service in the racially segregated military helped many immigrants in America become white. Prior to World War II, newer immigrants from places such as Italy and Ireland were seen as a separate race from other white immigrants. They were discriminated against and marginalized in society. In the American racial hierarchy, they were not seen as Blacks, but they were certainly not viewed as white. Because the military rigidly segregated its members by race as Black or white, ethnic groups such as Italians and Jews were put in white units, despite the fact that in the larger U.S. society, many considered them to be members of separate races. This helped cement their position in the white racial category. Whiteness and its associated privileges within the military, such as assignments to key units, shifted the racial boundaries to include more ethnic groups in the white category. This solidified the whiteness of these ethnic groups while simultaneously reaffirming the undesirability of Blackness.

There is no shortage of public memorials for veterans of World War II. After these veterans returned, the motivation for subsequent wars became less clear and the reception of veterans of those wars became more divided. However, for the boys who went off to World War II, the nation's gratitude has seemingly increased rather than abated over the decades. Every generation since has found ways to remember the sacrifice of this generation through parades and public memorials. Films have had a great influence in solidifying this laudatory view of the World War II generation. This well-worn narrative has been told many times without reference to its racial specificity and complexity, and over time it has become the "universal" story of that generation. Stanley Dunham's experiences fit well with that collection of narratives. The uniqueness of Stanley Dunham's story is that this white GI would raise the first Black president of the United States.

Obama's Commemoration of World War II

Many of Obama's discussions of his grandparents' experience in World War II took place at smaller gatherings and intimate campaign fund-raisers. At these events he often began his conversations as a way of connecting to audience members. He wanted to establish that he and the audience had something in common and that they shared this important historical memory. In most cases, he established the connection by pointing out attendees who were close to his grandparents' age. For instance, he began his remarks at a Veterans of Foreign Wars convention by relating to the World War II vets in the audience. He said, "For so many of you, like my grandfather, the original GI Bill changed your life—helping you to realize your dreams" (Obama 2009a). If he doesn't make a direct tie to people in the audience, he begins by taking a different route to the same arguments with statements such as, "So if I saw a couple that was 70 or 80, I'd think about my grandparents" (Obama 2012b). By recognizing people in the audience or referencing a previous generation, he is making a personal connection to others whose grandparents or parents (or even the person him or herself) may have had similar experiences. Indirectly, he is saying, "I am just like you. I am one of you."

After he establishes such connections, Obama goes on to give testimony about his grandparents' lives, which serve as an archetypal example of the lives of many men and women who served their country at home and abroad:

My grandfather enlisted after Pearl Harbor and went on to march in Patton's army. My grandmother worked on a bomber assembly line while he was gone. My mother was born at Ft. Leavenworth while he was away. When my grandfather returned he went to col-

lege on the GI Bill, he bought his first home from a loan from the
FHA [Federal Housing Administration]; moved his family west.
(Obama 2009b)

Many Baby Boomers know this story well because it was the story
of their parents who had lived it. They had come of age listening to
these stories and enjoying the benefits of their parents' sacrifices.
So when the president engaged them by invoking these memories,
he was affirming a particular narrative that for many Americans,
especially white Americans, is an example of American greatness
and a source of pride. He was establishing his membership in an
"imagined community" that sees its family history as one of unifying and noble patriotism (Anderson 2006).

Thus far, I have outlined two functions that Obama's World
War II narrative serves: establishing an authentic connection and
tapping into deep-felt emotions about national belonging and
sacrifice. It serves another function, too. The illustration the lives
of Stanley and Madelyn Dunham provide is also meant to convey a story of great American progress. In the post–World War
II era, the benefits given to returning veterans helped transform
American life and significantly increase the middle class. According to Edward Humes (2014), the GI Bill paid for the education
of "fourteen Nobel Prize winners, three Supreme Court justices,
three presidents, a dozen senators, two dozen Pulitzer Prize winners," and hundreds of thousands of teachers, doctors, lawyers,
engineers, and other middle-class professionals. Indeed, nearly
half of all students and three-fourths of all males enrolled in colleges in the fall of 1946 were veterans (Bennett 1996, 2). The rise
of planned communities such as Levittown, New York, and loans
guaranteed by the Veterans Administration made homeownership
possible for many families (Kushner 2010). Like these veterans

and their families, Stanley Dunham went to college and he and his wife bought a home and became a part of the burgeoning middle class. In Obama's accounts, there is no doubt that he sees their lives as laudable and heroic and that he feels that they had earned everything the government gave them in return. He acknowledges that government assistance to World War II veterans changed the economic trajectory of his family and many other families. Unfortunately, the sad complement to that story is the racially discriminatory policies that prevented African American veterans from taking full advantage of these programs.

The GI Bill aided veterans in two main areas—housing and education—that were also the sites of legal and informal segregation throughout the nation. Ira Katznelson (2006) suggests that this was America's first form of affirmative action policies because it was these programs that helped move many whites into the middle class. He offers a reframing of the notion of affirmative action to include policies such as the GI Bill—federal programs that targeted a specific race—and suggests that contemporary affirmative action policies should be seen in the same light as the federal programs of the New Deal and World War II. African American veterans benefited from the GI Bill and other programs to some extent, but the combined impact of discriminatory politics and racist practices severely limited their participation. Ta-Nehisi Coates (2014) says, "The oft-celebrated GI Bill . . . failed black Americans, by mirroring the broader country's insistence on a racist housing policy." For instance, banks were unwilling to give mortgage loans in Black communities, and much of the country adhered to formal and informal segregation (Callahan 2013). Racial zoning laws also allowed local communities to segregate on the basis of race through restrictive deeds and covenants (Rothstein 2014). Blacks were also unable to take advantage of postwar education benefits. While "43 percent of returning Black soldiers expressed a desire to enroll in school, their ability to do so was severely hampered by ongoing segregation in higher education: none of which the GI Bill did anything to reverse or prohibit" (Wise 2000). In the enormous transfer of wealth after World War II, white veterans and their families prospered, while Black veterans and their families did not.

In President Obama's estimation, his grandparents' tale emphasized a universal message of American exceptionalism for white audiences. It reinforces his familiar "only in America" refrain that when applied to his grandparents and, by extension, to himself demonstrates his improbable connection to a history that is almost always steeped in white imagery. This linkage between an important moment of patriotic whiteness and an African American candidate had the potential to make him more palatable to white voters who would be leery of him otherwise. Obama reiterated the democratic ideology upon which white American patriotism is built. He said, "My grandfather came back home and that generation got the GI Bill. That was great for *everyone* because it upgraded the skills of all *our* workers, that wasn't just good for some, *that was good for all*" (Obama 2012a; italics added). Notice that Obama stated that all people should see the GI Bill as a positive benefit, regardless of its discriminatory character. This unqualified statement allows whites to maintain their unblemished view of American democracy. Sadly, it also asks African Americans, his greatest supporters and the constituency that was key to his electoral coalition, to go along with what Harris (2012) calls "wink-and-nod" politics. Obama asked Blacks to be complicit in this distorted account of the past by continuing their support for him. At the same time, he asked them to rely on and trust his ability to make future policies less exclusionary and more just.

Blacks, War, and Citizenship

For African Americans, World War II is not a simple story of patriotism and sacrifice, although they had an enormous amount of both. Their service to the country was fraught with serious and legitimate crises of conscience. Should Blacks sign up for the opportunity to fight for the freedom of others when the freedom of most African Americans was fragile and severely constricted? Life experience had instilled in them a deep critique of America's democratic promise. They knew that that freedom had been built on the backs of enslaved Africans and their descendants and that Blacks had been systematically excluded from the benefits of citizenship. However, as Stephen Marshall (2011) has aptly demonstrated, African Americans possess a "prophetic vision" of the possibilities of American democracy. They have the capacity to see beyond their decidedly anti-democratic experiences in America and understand the potential freedom that undergirds the stated goals of the U.S. Constitution.

World War II was not the first time Blacks had debated whether or not they should fight for a country that had long denied them basic rights. For many Black Americans, the discrimination and violence they had experienced with the tacit and explicit consent of local, state, and federal governments made swearing allegiance to the nation and potentially sacrificing one's life for it difficult at best. More so than questions about Black allegiance to America, the decision of whether or not to serve in the military conjured a Du Boisian dual consciousness whereby "one ever feels his two-ness—an American, a Negro; two souls, two thoughts, two unreconciled strivings; two warring ideals in one dark body, whose dogged strength alone keeps it from being torn asunder" (Du Bois [1918] 2000a, 222). Deciding to join the military or obey draft laws is a decision to put one's life at risk for the ideals of one's nation, and when those ideals have remained beyond the reach of your group, that decision is far more complex.

Historically, Black leaders have positioned military service as a pathway to increased rights. They argued that Blacks would prove themselves deserving of full citizenship rights by demonstrating their patriotism. In 1863, in an effort to recruit Black soldiers during the Civil War, Fredrick Douglass ([1863] 2000, 525) warned Blacks in his piece "Men of Color, To Arms!" that if they didn't fight then, "liberty won by white men would lose half its luster." The meaning of liberty would be diminished for Blacks because they would not have participated in attaining those rights, Douglass argued, and whites would be quick to note their unwillingness to fight. Thus, enlisting served a dual purpose for the future of Blacks in America. In this same speech, Douglass said: "This is a golden opportunity—let us accept it—and forever wipe out the dark reproaches unsparingly hurled against us by our enemies; win for ourselves gratitude of our Country and the best blessings of our posterity through all time" (527). African American elites reiterated this argument during both world wars. In their opinion, military service would be the most public demonstration of patriotism and an indisputable sign of national loyalty.

Beyond encouraging mass enlistments, Black leaders also saw wartime as a time to set aside grievances. Loyalty during war was about more than a call to new action. It required an embargo on old actions such as protest and critique. In a 1918 essay called "Closing Ranks," W. E. B. Du Bois ([1903] 2000b, 243) admonished those who wanted to boycott and those who advocated enlistment when he suggested that "while the war lasts, forget our special grievances and close our ranks shoulder to shoulder with our white fellow citizens and allied nations fighting for democracy."

In 1918, these special grievances were numerous and widespread. Lynching and other forms of state-sanctioned and state-tolerated violence and racially aggressive policies were making life for Blacks immensely difficult (Wells [1913] 2014; Berg 2011). According to a report on lynching by the Equal Justice Initiative (2015, 5), "'terror lynching' peaked between 1880 and 1940 and claimed the lives of African American men, women, and children who were forced to endure the fear, humiliation, and barbarity of this widespread phenomenon unaided." African Americans searched for ways to comprehend and cope with these vicious events. African American leaders investigated lynching incidents and lobbied the federal government on behalf of victimized citizens (Giddings 2009; Gaines 2007). African Americans also used other media to inform their community about issues that threatened it. Koritha Mitchell (2011) highlights the popularity of lynching plays that were published and produced for Black audiences. Mitchell points to the use of the soldier as a main character because soldiers, like doctors and lawyers, were considered model Black citizens. Soldiers who were lynched in uninform were a particular paradox for African Americans because despite the fact that they wore the uniform that symbolized service and sacrifice, they were still victims of racially targeted violence.

Until the mid-1960s, most veterans were locked out of the voting booth and were excluded from any political participation that might lead to lasting policies. Despite this, Du Bois and other leaders asked Blacks to ignore such circumstances and focus on future possibilities. They argued that military service was an investment in achieving an equality that was currently being denied the Black community. During World War II, Black newspapers promoted the Double-V Campaign, which argued that if African Americans enlisted in significant numbers, there would be "victory over our enemies at home and victory over our enemies on the battlefields abroad" (Bailey and Farber 1993, 817). Initiated by the *Pittsburgh Courier* and eventually adopted by the entire Black press, social justice organizations, and Black religious and fraternal organizations, this campaign promised increased equality for returning veterans and, by extension, for all Blacks (Hohn 2008; Simpson 1994). Enlisting was a demonstration of patriotism and loyalty to the American democratic project. Robert J. Norrell (2005, 123) notes that despite concerns about inequality at home, "one million blacks put on uniforms and served their country" during World War II. Those who served reminded white Americans and the world that they were as committed to the goals of democracy as their white counterparts were.

There were clear internationalist arguments for why Black soldiers deserved and should be given more respect during and after the war. In an essay called "The Negro Soldier," Charles Hamilton Houston ([1994] 2000, 340) pointed out that America's treatment of Blacks was detrimental to the nation's effort to present itself as a model of a free society for the rest of the world. He noted, "The American color bar unless speedily removed will be the rock on which our international Good Neighbor policy and our pious claim to moral leadership will flounder." Houston understood clearly that many Americans believed that American-style democracy was better than communism and that this notion could easily be called into doubt by examining the experiences of African Americans. Black newspapers and leaders of the period attempted to make arguments that linked fascism in Europe with domestic racism. In addition, the actions of Black soldiers who had helped liberate vulnerable citizens in Europe would simultaneously demonstrate the need for liberation at home. Proponents of Black participation in the war also articulated a connection between Black soldiers' liberation efforts (internationally and domestically) and the budding liberation movements on the African continent in the period leading up to World War II (Gaines 2007).

Although African American soldiers were discriminated against by their fellow soldiers and citizens, they served with the expectation that life after the war would be better for them individually and for their entire community. Christopher Parker (2009, 5) asserts that "black veterans' willingness to challenge white supremacy and resist Jim Crow rested to a significant extent upon their military experience." Arguing against the belief that military service makes soldiers more conservative, Parker found that returning Black veterans were more likely to engage in protest behavior than Blacks who did not serve. Veterans' service enabled them to see themselves as full members of the American political community, increased their sense of agency, and developed the commitment and confidence needed to fight white supremacy. The hopefulness their service had engendered and the disappointment with their treatment after the war instilled in Black veterans a desire to fight segregationist policies in the same way that they had fought fascist policies abroad.

For whites, national service was and continues to be bound up in duty and patriotism. Indeed, a sense of obligation to country is part of what creates and sustains national loyalty. National service is about a sense of duty and loyalty for African Americans too; however, for them, national service has also been entangled with a need to demonstrate their worthiness to be included in the American political process. In highlighting his grandparents' service, Obama underscores his personal history as a descendant of a white GI, with all the benefits that entailed. He does not qualify his statements by saying that his white grandfather is the veteran he is referring to and that his whiteness matters for the story he tells. Instead, he is an African American man touting the benefits of a white experience. What audiences see is an African American discussing post–World War II programs for veterans as if all racial groups benefited from them in similar ways. They did not, and without proper racial context Obama's narrative serves to both reinforce and laud his familial legacy and at the same time erase the legacy of struggle by members of his racial group. His telling of the story without important caveats implies racial universality where it does not exist. The soldiers who looked like him were denied the progress of this period. President Obama has inherited a form of patriotic whiteness that is inaccessible to most Blacks. It is not required that he deny that inheritance, but the way he presents it should be done with great care so that it does not inadvertently bolster claims of white privilege.

Patriotic Whiteness

Barack Obama employs the narrative of patriotic whiteness under specific conditions. He did not just evoke his grandparents' story erratically or irreverently; instead, he used it strategically to engage with audiences for whom this narrative resonates in an important way. He was judicious about deciding which stories were best given to particular audiences. We clearly see in this case that Obama understands the nuanced ways that patriotism can be evoked and how the narratives related to patriotism can be heavily dependent on race. When he accesses the patriotic sentiments of white audiences, he mentions his grandparents and their membership in the greatest generation. In contrast, when he speaks to Blacks, he is more likely to point to the civil rights movement as a model of Black patriotism. This realization leads to important conclusions about his use of his grandparents' life story.

First, Obama did not use his grandparents' experience in an exploitative way. He did not inappropriately reach for ways to incorporate his grandparents' story by mentioning it at every campaign stop. He refrained from discussing this story with people for whom it would be politically and emotionally irrelevant—such as members of the millennial generation, for example. In fact, he did not even mention it every time he talked to veterans, in contexts where it would be wholly appropriate and expected. He primarily broached the subject in service of larger narratives and more specific political goals. He brought it up when he was campaigning and needed support from people for whom the narrative is salient. He brought it up in situations where he wanted to demonstrate America's ability to reach increasingly higher goals by tearing down obstacles. He asked members of his audience to think about this narrative as historically important because it invokes positive sentiments about America's past actions but also acts as a guide for his current desire to enact redistributive policies such as the expansion of access to health care. For him to become president in 2008, for him to govern since, for him to be seen as presidential, he needed Americans to believe that electing him was a continuation of that exceptional World War II story. Like the whites in the audience, he had inherited an understanding of the power of service and sacrifice to the nation. He was willing to volunteer for duty, using the tools—in the form of shared values—that had shaped them all as they heard the stories of their parents and grandparents. For the success of the narrative to work as a tool for recruiting supports, those being persuaded had to believe that electing him was part of a national lineage, not an entire upheaval of a system. Electing this Black candidate was not the creation of a new order but a continuation of what his grandparents and their grandparents had accomplished and planned for their future generations.

Second, and relatedly, President Obama talked about this aspect of his personal history almost exclusively to majority-white or veteran audiences and rarely mentioned it to Black audiences. His reasons for sharing this with veterans are obvious. All candidates and political figures seek votes and approval by finding ways to have a more identifiable appeal to constituent groups. Thus, when a politician is with veterans, she should talk about war, service, and sacrifice. If the politician has not served, then relying on the stories of his or her parents and grandparents makes the most sense. Why Obama decided to reserve his narrative of family service for majority-white audiences is less straightforward. Surely during his two campaigns there were people in majority-Black audiences who were in their "70s and 80s" or who were his grandparents' ages, but when speaking to such audiences, he did not refer to their military service. Instead, he pointed to more recent civil rights struggles and spoke about pathology within Black culture. The reference to the civil rights movement does similar work as the World War II story. They are both historical efforts that became emblematic of the best of American idealism.

Obama's decision to use specific narratives with specific groups based on race created a juxtaposition in which white soldiers, specifically his grandfather and other World War II veterans, put their life on the line for global freedom, and Blacks, specifically civil rights activists, put their lives on the line so Blacks could vote and make better life choices. This tendency to use the World War II narrative only for white audiences may be the result of what he believes Black audiences expect to hear or what he thinks they should hear. It is likely a combination of both, but the result is that his decisions enforce the notion that patriotism as demonstrated through military service is a primarily white project. Sacrifice for whites is grand and universal; sacrifice for Blacks is basic citizenship and personal moral responsibilities. As was the case with their experiences in World War II and other important military moments in American history, the experiences of African Americans are either sidelined or rendered invisible.

Last, Obama harkens back to the birth of a post–World War II white middle class that served as the foundation for the successes for many of his contemporaries. His narrative also represented the possibility that a nation that was currently engaged in wars on multiple fronts could emerge from it more successful than it was before, as was the case for America after World War II. He provided a template for success by pointing to a particular past, and by noting his connection to that past, and he indicated his understanding of what made that past so laudable and what made him a suitable leader who could usher in a new and similarly prosperous era. It was a beloved past that symbolized an idyllic America that in many ways is seen as the standard for future generations. His reliance on this story put him in league with people who transformed the world by taking risks, and his narrative expressed his hope that current voters would take similar risks by changing the tide of history regarding race and the presidency. It asked the beneficiaries of the "greatest generation" to see him as a one of them instead of focusing on how his Blackness would make voting for him as president a clear departure. His narrative emphasized that he is among the progeny of the greatest generation.

3

Barack Obama's More Perfect Union

While Black feminist scholars have long drawn parallels between developments in civil rights and women's rights mobilizations and have called attention to the intricate intersections of racism and sexism, mainstream discussions of Black politics have remained insulated from these insights (Crenshaw 1991). By bringing together discussions of the meaning and import of postracialism and the nature and scope of postfeminism, it is possible to comprehend how certain forms of race and gender privilege animate discussions that prioritize the experiences of the individual and diminish those of groups of which that individual might be a member. Here, I draw upon Rebecca Clark Mane's (2012) analysis of the "syntaxes of whiteness" that permeate third-wave feminist arguments to illuminate the fact that similar racial dynamics operate in Barack Obama's historic 2008 speech "A More Perfect Union." I begin with a comparison of various "waves" of African American and women's activism, demonstrating parallels between claims about postracialism and postfeminism. I am not arguing that these waves map neatly onto one another. Rather, I argue that changes in emphasis, argumentation, and tactics in both of these cultural developments have strong similarities that are worth exploring. I then use Mane's analysis of four "grammars of whiteness" to analyze Obama's 2008 treatise on race and U.S. race relations. I conclude the chapter with some comments on what Obama's framing of race means for race and gender scholars and for activists who continue to rely on identity frames to make group-based demands.

The election of Barack Obama fueled many discussions about the dawn of a postracial epoch in which ascriptive categories no longer overdetermined our lives. In a feature article in the *New York Times Magazine*, Matt Bai (2008) suggested that Obama's cross-racial appeal signaled "The End of Black Politics." Characterizing Obama as a member of a new generation of Black politicians who "have challenged their elders in traditionally black districts," Bai claimed that the president's election marked the culmination of the long struggle for equal citizenship. He derided "the old guard" for failing to "come to terms . . . with the success of their struggle . . . and [embracing] the idea that black politics might now be disappearing." At the very least, Bai insisted, President Obama's election marked the end of group-based politics modeled on the categories and norms of the protest movements of the 1960s. He argued that in exploding the limits of group boundaries, Barack Obama symbolized the triumph of individualized identity that transcended the constraints of race. Interestingly, it is unclear that civil rights activists and others saw race as the problem. For them, the problem was not Blackness (as a racial category) but white supremacy as a system of domination.

The story of race in the age of Obama is decidedly more intricate. Although Obama won enough votes to secure the presidency, the voting results lagged behind public opinion polls, suggesting that a lesser version of the Bradley effect may have been in operation.[1] Noting a gap between Obama's popularity in public opinion polls and the percentages who voted for him in the 2008 presidential election, some voting scholars suggest that Obama would have won by an even larger margin that year if white votes had matched projections in opinion polls (Lewis-Beck, Tien, and Nadeau 2010). McCormick and Jones (1993) have long noted that African American candidates have to grapple with persistent racial stereotypes by avoiding personal traits negatively associated with Blackness and issues that invoke racial ideations. They must champion race-neutral policy proposals and studiously avoid race-conscious policies. Race also operates in campaigns tactically; both major political parties have intentionally exploited whites' racial fears to give white candidates an advantage (Haney López 2014; Mendelberg 2001). Black candidates have to negotiate the complexities of racial bias and racist preferences to craft successful campaigns. Their stated campaign rhetoric may be devoid of race talk, but their underlying campaign strategy is scaffold by concerns about race.

Given the continuing significance of race in American life, how should we situate the claims regarding a "postracial" era, and how does Barack Obama figure in postracial discourses? "Postracialism" is a term that has been bandied about in popular media, although the way it is defined is often contradictory and inconsistent. For many, "postracial" means that race is no longer a defining feature in the American social and political landscape. For some, postracialism represents the obsolescence of ascriptive categories. Shedding racial group identity as a defining characteristic can also entail release from communal obligations and freedom to prioritize, pursue, and achieve individual goals. For others, the postracial moment enables a reordering rather than a rejection of group-based identities. According to Touré (2011, 12), postblack actors are "leaving behind the visions of Blackness as something narrowly definable and embracing every conception of Blackness as legitimate." In his calculation, it is Blacks who have created a limited vision of Blackness, and millennials are now able to break free from these limitations. Is Obama, then, a harbinger of a new era or the beneficiary of an ongoing transformation?

This chapter seeks to understand the contemporary turn towards postracialism in the context of the larger debate over the nature of this "post-identity" moment (postblack, postfeminist, postnation, etc.) that many suggest we are currently experiencing.[2] What can we make of claims that our various and multiple group identities no longer define the life experiences and outcomes of individual members? Various strands of scholarship have suggested that the twenty-first century has finally fulfilled the promise of liberal individualism: they argue that individual achievement and self-actualization now determine outcomes because the burdens and baggage of past histories of discrimination and oppression associated with particular groups have been eliminated. This optimistic assessment has gained significant traction in media outlets that have a tendency to focus on certain accomplishments and victories as the outcome of past struggles rather than focusing on contemporary struggles. In this view, lengthy civil disobedience campaigns by people of color, women, veterans, and other groups have ushered in significant electoral, judicial, and legislative reforms.[3] In this view, explicit discriminatory policies and practices that targeted specific racial, sexual, and gender minorities in earlier eras have been removed from legal language, public norms, and social expression. For many proponents of post-identity theories, the changes since the 1960s and 1970s indicate that the social ills that activists of those decades were fighting against have been successfully eliminated. Precisely because of these victories, contemporary generations can now focus on developing and nurturing personal identities free of past limitations and free of any feelings of obligation to their identity group.

This optimism is misplaced. What is interpreted as post-identity has far less to do with the elimination of the biases associated with marginalized identities than with a shift to a subtle and amorphous form of discrimination in contemporary society that makes the presence and dynamics of these biases harder to capture (Bonilla-

Silva 2006). Without careful interrogation, success stories such as Barack Obama's ascendency to the presidency can overshadow the mechanisms of continuing exclusion, making identity-centered discrimination particularly difficult to demonstrate.[4] In this chapter, I bring these mechanisms out of the shadows by demonstrating similarities between postrace and postfeminist scholarship. I also point to the ways post-identity movements make claims of connections to previous identity-based movements while at the same time discounting the need for their continued existence and reinforcing claims that support and uphold the current racial order.

Postracial, Postfeminist: Thinking through and beyond the Waves

Periodizing history is a particularly fraught endeavor. Although fixing the boundaries of historical epochs is the stock in trade of historians, political scientists have also grappled with questions about what constitutes a "watershed" period, when one era is ending (e.g., the New Deal, the civil rights movement) and something altogether new is on the horizon. It has been a convention in women's historiography to demarcate three "waves" of women's rights activism. Although there has been intensive contestation over the adequacy of the wave metaphor to capture the activism of various segments of feminist movements (Hewitt 2010a), conventional usage has given concrete meaning to particular social and political mobilizations that focus on strategies and tactics employed, participation in organizations, popular support, and specific policy goals. By convention, "first-wave feminism" encompassed the longest era of feminist history in America and was characterized by women's prolonged fight for basic recognition as full legal citizens and access to the ballot (Hewitt 2010b). The "second wave" is typically associated with the women's movement and the protest politics of the 1960s, 1970s, and 1980s, which moved beyond formal equality and focused on the law as a mechanism of social transformation. This mass movement sought to bring about a transformation of values, equal participation in all areas of American life, reproductive freedom, and bodily integrity. The chronology and the content of the "third wave" have been subjects of much debate (Snyder 2008). Third-wave feminists are grappling with the contradictions that arise when feminism is moved from the academy to the streets. They see themselves as having and taking advantage of multiple (albeit complicated) personal and professional choices made available to them by the gains of the previous waves. Relying on personal narratives as the ingredients of theory building, they seek to give voice to cross-cutting differences, thereby underscoring the complexity of womanhood. Third-wave feminists view themselves as full beneficiaries of the efforts of previous generations of feminists to dismantle legal and social barriers. Precisely because those battles have been fought and won, third-wave women are able to chart their own courses, free of constraints from external actors and expectations that circumscribed their feminist foremothers' lives.

Astrid Henry (2004, 21) argues that third-wave feminism is shaped by "at least three distinct, albeit interconnected concepts: generational age, ideological position, and historical moment." Women espousing this ideological viewpoint represent younger feminists' rejection of what they see as the rigidity of second-wave feminism. In her pioneering edited volume *To Be Real*, Rebecca Walker (1995, xxxiv) suggests that the volume contributors (all of whom were third wavers) "have done the difficult work of being real (refusing to be bound by a feminist ideal not of their own making) and telling the truth (honoring the complexity and contradictions in their lives by adding their experiences to the feminist dialogue)." Third-wave feminist scholars depict themselves as open and inclusive, suggesting that they encompass all "strains" of feminism, however contradictory, creating a "hybrid kind that perhaps . . . [needs] a different name altogether" (Haywood and Drake 2006, 25).

The boundaries between the first, second, and third feminist waves are by no means rigid. Black feminist scholars, for instance, have noted that wave analogies often poorly account for the chronologies of Black feminist activism (Springer 2002).[5] Some younger Black feminists, such as hip-hop feminists, see a commonality with third-wave feminism, but "hip-hop feminism rejects the staunch politics of generation disavowal so prevalent in most third-wave feminist work" (Durham, Cooper, and Morris 2013, 723; see also Peoples 2008). Although the wave metaphor has porous boundaries, it facilitates reference to broad historical periods. Even as battles for rights and recognition continue, these overarching descriptions paint a picture of the U.S. feminist movement—and creative appropriation of the wave chronology is helpful in framing discussions of race and politics. The wave metaphor captures historical context and dimensions of social change in political movements and communities, and it can help historicize Black politics, illuminating internal shifts related to tactics, strategies, and perspectives.

Throughout much of American political history, the pursuit of gender equality has paralleled and at times mapped directly onto the quest for racial justice. Black activism and women's rights activism are related by more than a common desire to end group-based oppression; their related social movements were also constituted by many of the same activists (Brienes 2006; McAdam 1988). Extrapolating from feminist chronologies, we can divide Black politics into three waves. The first wave of Black politics starts with the pursuit of emancipation and legal recognition as human be-ings and American citizens. This includes the political work of abolitionists and others to secure freedom and citizenship rights for Blacks (Franklin and Moss 2000). The second wave of Black politics is marked by the civil rights movement, mass protests, and legal battles that revolutionized U.S. race relations and influenced subsequent civil rights movements around the globe.[6] The transi-tion from the civil rights movement to contemporary politics is often called the movement from protest to politics (Rustin 2003). The passage of the Voting Rights Act in 1965 represented a turn toward a narrow focus on the vote as a singular path to Black po-litical empowerment. The combination of the Voting Rights Act and urban white flight created a political base that elected many urban-based Black officials. Many of those first politicians (e.g., Maynard Jackson, Coleman Young, Sharpe James, and Marion Barry) were civil rights movement veterans who translated the tactics they learned in protest movements into governing styles (Johnson 2007; Tate 1993; Nelson and Merranto 1977).

Despite the damaging impact of white flight on urban econo-mies, second-wave mayors were able to achieve large-scale growth. By developing relationships with business leaders and combining firebrand rhetoric and public protest, these early Black elected of-ficials cultivated extremely loyal constituencies. In the twenty-first century, however, most of the insurgent-style politicians have been successfully challenged and supplanted by younger candidates who lack a connection to the protests of the 1960s (Gillespie 2012). Similar to third-wave feminists, although much less contentious as a group, Blacks in the post–civil rights era are able to take ad-vantage of civil rights gains and electoral opportunities. With the growth of a significant Black middle class that was made possible by increased access to education and professional occupations, African Americans are no longer barred from the mainstream political process. Conceiving of themselves as the beneficiaries of the civil rights struggle, many among this new generation of African Americans believe that times have changed. Released from the racial baggage of the past, they anticipate unencumbered progress. In this new postracial context, they pursue elective office with the support of white and Black voters by crafting issue positions that explicitly avoid discussions of race and race-related issues. They run deracialized campaigns (McCormick and Jones 1993).

Comparing the trajectories of African American and feminist movements fruitfully illuminates several common features. The first and most obvious ground for comparison is the presence of many of the same actors in these movements for extended periods of time. Overlapping constituencies can be traced to nineteenth-century efforts by prominent activists such as Fredrick Douglass, Sojourner Truth, and Lucretia Mott on behalf of both abolition and women's rights. Connections can also be found in mid-twentieth-century collaborations among members of the Student Non-Violent Coordinating Committee such as Casey Hayden and Mary King, whose signal memo penned during the 1964 Freedom Summer Project encapsulated the experiences of women doing racial justice work in Mississippi (Brienes 2006; Foner 1992; McMillen 2009). In addition to overlapping actors, both groups fought for many of the same goals and demands, including legal recognition of personhood, access to the ballot, and other basic rights that were the exclusive possession of white men, as well as more freedom and autonomy over not just their own lives but their own bodies. Both groups used the courts and mass protest to make demands that institutions and government officials change laws and policies regarding individual control over their corporeal selves, over who represented them politically, and over access to social, educational, and political institutions. These parallels in first- and second-wave goals, strategies, and accomplishments provide good reason to expect continuing similarities in the contemporary postracial, postfeminist moment.

Third-wave feminist writing and Barack Obama's political ascendency unfolded in the same social context. They emerge after sustained and large-scale protests challenged the legal and social structures that had overtly prohibited gender and racial equality. Their second-wave forebearers can boast of important accomplishments. Biased policies that explicitly targeted certain identity groups were removed in favor of race-neutral and gender-neutral language, stronger enforcement of anti-discrimination policies by the Justice Department and other federal agencies, and local laws banning race and gender discrimination. Plaintiffs and advocacy groups established legal precedence for equality claims through cases such as *Brown v. Board of Education* and *Roe v. Wade* and created a climate in which overt expressions of intolerance are viewed as socially unacceptable. While these changes have not eradicated sexism or racism, they have changed the terrain upon which groups pursue equality claims. Both Obama and contemporary race and gender scholars undertake their work in the era of multiculturalism that champions "diversity" as the optimal social structure. In this era, race-neutral language creates the veneer of equality, even as policies that produce racially and gender biased results continue to be created (e.g., welfare reform, third-strike laws).

Yet this celebration of individualism coexists with a prolonged and concerted effort by conservatives to roll back many civil rights gains under the guise of states' rights and claims of reverse racism that co-opt equal protection arguments. In the wake of this conservative backlash, many policies have been either dismantled completely or rendered toothless (Steinberg 1995).[7] In this complex environment, racial and gender discrimination assume a more nebulous character. Infractions of rights are harder to detect and even harder to defend against. Barack Obama's quest for the presidency emerged during this period of ambiguity. Scholars, pundits, and citizens agreed that Obama's victory signaled a game change in electoral politics and potentially, in the larger society. Some claimed that the legacy of the civil rights era had reached its natural end and that Martin Luther King's dream of individuals being judged by the "content of their character" had been largely achieved. Obama was consistently referred to as a "race transcendent" candidate (Will 2007; Helman 2007; Rivers 2008; Goldberg 2008).

Similarly, gender no longer plays the constraining role that it once did. The battles first- and second-wave feminists fought and won over the rights of women to make independent choices in their own lives have ushered in a new era. Coming of age in a period of expanded opportunity, women of the third wave are free to flout the changes in gender norms and the policy gains made by the previous generations. Again Touré (2011, 12) is instructive. He suggests that in the Obama era, "postblack" means being "rooted in but not restricted to Blackness." By analogy, "postfeminist" means rooted in but not restricted by feminism. Thus, a 2005 article in the *New York Times Magazine* reported that an increasing number of women at elite universities "say they will happily play a traditional female role, with motherhood their main commitment" (Story 2005).[8] In opposition to their feminist forebears, who challenged gender roles and the boundaries created by traditional social norms, these women view their choices as unrestrained and declare themselves free to follow their hearts wherever they may lead. For those who embrace this postrace, postfeminist moment, individual self-actualization is the hallmark of their new freedom, and they distinguish themselves from previous generations by embracing more fluid identities that blur and challenge previous norms.

Those who believe that there has been a shift in American race relations since the civil rights era insist that racist sentiments have greatly decreased. There is some evidence to support this claim. For several decades, whites have been more reluctant to express overtly racist views about African Americans than they had been in previous generations. Although this does not mean that whites no longer engage in racial stereotyping or have ceased to hold old-fashioned racist views, public opinion polls find that respondents are less likely to express overtly racist views and instead tend to provide more socially desirable responses (Kinder and Sanders 1996; Sniderman and Piazza 1993). The rise of multiculturalism and diversity outreach programs changed the face of many institutions and interactions in America.[9] These efforts resulted in real gains in American race relations. What individuals mean when they say they want "diversity" is a subject of intense debate, but it is indisputable that individuals, organizations, and institutions express a desire for diversity.

A more cynical interpretation of recent changes in race and gender debates in America suggests a silencing of white supremacist and male supremacist views rather than an eradication of these sentiments. Because overtly racist and, to some extent, sexist expression is now deemed inappropriate, those who hold such views have been forced underground. Public declarations of beliefs about Black and female inferiority have been replaced by subtler forms of racism and sexism that couch support for racial discrimination in "doubts" about "shared values" and masked appeals to race- and sex-neutral policies. For example, discrimination against women is shrouded in discussions of respectability politics and appropriate attire and behavior (Higginbotham 1993; see also Cooper 2012). Similarly, Eduardo Bonilla-Silva (2006) has demonstrated in his aptly titled book *Racism without Racists* that even in the face of contradictory and discriminatory statements about Blacks, whites still insist that they are not racists. "Whites rationalize minorities' contemporary status as the product of market dynamics, naturally-occurring phenomena, and blacks' imputed cultural limitations" (Bonilla-Silva 2006, 2). When there are no racists, there are no grounds for racial grievances to be adjudicated. Under such circumstances, "postracialism" and "postfeminism" simply mask a hostile environment in which it is increasingly difficult to call out incidents of racism and misogyny. Barack Obama never overtly endorses the positions of post-identity proponents. Instead, he seems to believe that racism continues to exist but to a significantly diminished degree. As a result, his arguments sometimes connect neatly with post-identity tenets. For African Americans, who see Obama's identity as a Black man as a critical factor in the importance of his election, post-identity arguments are not appealing. In addition, African Americans continue to view themselves and make claims based on their group identity. If the person they support emphasizes individualism over groups, their votes may not lead to the policy outcomes they desire.

Obama and the Third Wave

In many ways Barack Obama is a quintessential third-wave figure. He relies heavily on his identity and personal narrative as a signifier for his right to belong. His connection to Blackness *and* whiteness blurs racial boundaries and provides the foundation for his political bona fides and moral uprightness. Most of what Americans know about him and his "authentic" political beliefs stems from his two best-selling memoirs and his speech at the 2004 Democratic National Convention (Obama 2004a, 2004b, 2008a). His life and his presidency embody racial advancements. And his one address about race during the 2008 campaign resonates with third-wave rhetoric.

Obama's (2008b) "A More Perfect Union" speech at the National Constitution Center in Philadelphia on March 18, 2008, is the only statement he has made on race as a candidate. It is the most cogent and direct expression of his vision of the role of race and racial history in American society. It also offers important insights into the possibilities for American race relations in the twenty-first century. Barack Obama was pressured into addressing the topic of race. He gave this speech in response to claims that Jeremiah Wright, his pastor for more than two decades, was both anti-white and anti-American. The scene itself was powerful not just because of the row of American flags that served as a backdrop while he spoke, but also because of the politically sacred ground upon which he chose to make his stand. The National Constitution Center shares a mall with Independence Hall, where both the Declaration of Independence and the Constitution were drafted, debated, and proclaimed. Both of these documents reduced the personhood of those who shared Obama's race to property. The speech was broadcast on all networks and received over a million views on YouTube. It was the most watched event of the 2008 campaign. According to the Pew Research Center (2008), a full 85 percent of Americans said they had heard "a little about the speech" and 54 percent said they had heard "a lot."

Obama, who wrote the speech himself, began by noting the history of the venue and all the racial history that came with it.

After a discussion of slavery and its continuing impact on the nation, he began to speak about his own family's racial diversity and what that taught him about race. He was clear about distancing himself from Rev. Wright, but he also used that discussion as a starting point to outline his view of African Americans' sentiments regarding race, whites' anger and resentment, and prescriptions for a more harmonious future. Like many campaign speeches, he ended with a heartwarming personal story about racial unity on the campaign trail. There was widespread reaction to his address. Supporters lauded it as a masterful triumph and detractors derided it as smoke and mirrors. Regardless of perspective, it was viewed by all as a pivotal moment in the campaign.

As in many of his public talks, Obama positions himself in "A More Perfect Union" as the quintessential emblem of the new postracial order. Like many third-wavers, he celebrates his ability to throw off group constraints in order to forge a new "way" of being. By looking "to personal experiences to provide knowledge about how the world operates and to trouble dominant narratives about how things should be" (Snyder 2008, 184), his personal narrative becomes a central signpost of post-identity living. Identifying himself as a complex individual, Obama embraces a wide array of identity positions.

> I am the son of a black man from Kenya and a white woman from Kansas. I was raised with the help of a white grandfather who survived a Depression to serve in Patton's Army during World War II and a white grandmother who worked on a bomber assembly line at Fort Leavenworth while he was overseas. I've gone to some of the best schools in America and lived in one of the world's poorest nations. I am married to a black American who carries within her the blood of slaves and slave-owners—an inheritance we pass

on to our two precious daughters. I have brothers, sisters, nieces, nephews, uncles and cousins, of every race and every hue, scattered across three continents, and for as long as I live, I will never forget that in no other country on earth is my story even possible. (Obama 2008b)

Obama presents his freedom to be an individual as a consequence of both the heroic struggles of previous generations, and his unique location in the United States, where the constraints of identity no longer hold sway. Like other third-wave figures, Obama claims to have learned from the mistakes of his forebears and to have designed his politics and policies to avoid replicating those mistakes. From Kenya to Kansas and across three continents, his life is marked by difference and diversity, always framed within a larger context of equality. "A More Perfect Union" is emblematic of third-wave rhetoric. For this reason, it is a particularly useful place to begin to reflect on tacit messages that raise serious questions about this postracial moment.

The Syntaxes of Whiteness and Obama's Views on Race

In "Transmuting Grammars of Whiteness in Third-Wave Feminism," Rebecca Clark Mane (2012, 71) provides an insightful analysis of "whiteness" as a structuring ideology that permeates third-wave texts. Though the arguments of third-wave feminists are intended to move beyond previous generations' emphasis on equality and injustices, they employ four "syntaxes of whiteness" that produce, secure, and maintain—rather than transform or transcend—the current racial order. Despite the fact that third-wave proponents acknowledge and discuss difference often, Mane suggests that upon closer examination, these appeals to diversity replicate a naturalized and unspoken set of relations that privileges whites. Instead of accepting professed commitments to equality at face value, Mane points out that reading against the grain can demonstrate how inclusiveness and marginalization co-exist within the same rhetoric. "Third-wave texts reveal a set of structuring grammars of whiteness . . . that allow for the proliferation of difference . . . while simultaneously containing and sublimating the discomforting dangers of racial and national intersectionalities" (72). Simply put, diversity talk is cheap when the language used also supports continued white privilege.

Mane conceptualizes whiteness as a system of knowing that shapes perceptions in ways that exclude ideas, beliefs, or evidence that is contrary to white interests. The grammars of whiteness are purportedly "innocent and natural ways of organizing perceptions" that have the "potential to infiltrate and colonize even progressive discourses" (74–75). Four of these organizing devices, or "syntaxes of whiteness," surface regularly in third-wave texts. The first syntax of whiteness is intimately tied to the temporality of the postracial, postfeminist era. Third-wavers routinely identify with the critical interventions of feminists of color who generated so many powerful analyses of second-wave feminism. They position themselves as anti-racist proponents of absolute equality. Yet their conceptions of the harms of racial injustice and sexual inequality are always situated in the past. For them, the project of equality has been accomplished and it is time to move on. According to Mane, framing racial and gender inequity as problems long-solved places contemporary injustice below the threshold of visibility and beyond redress.

Mane positions the second syntax of whiteness in relation to what Roland Barthes calls the "privation of history" (quoted in Mane 2012, 79). Third-wavers discuss inequalities without placing them in any historical context. Deprived of adequate contextualization, specific injustices are disconnected from the systemic problems that produced them. In the absence of clear causation, injustices float free and lack a clear path to reparation. Without a clear cause and a strategy to fix the problem, inequalities exist as abstractions with no ties to contemporary practices.

In the absence of historical context, contemporary relevance, and a sense of an urgent need to redress problems, inequalities are converted into "difference" and "diversity." Precisely because they have been raised to value diversity, third-wavers fail to recognize that difference can indicate pernicious hierarchies of power. If all differences are equally valued, important ethical distinctions are flattened out. Modes of marginalization that entail severe constriction of individual life prospects become indistinguishable from trivial differences that carry no moral weight. In a moral frame that values all differences equally, it becomes impossible to discern benign from invidious distinctions. Hence, the strategies required to rectify systemic racial and gender discrimination become indistinguishable from "reverse discrimination."

Mane (2012, 85) suggests that the final syntax of whiteness is embedded in third-wavers' acceptance of "irreconcilable contradictions." Many third-wavers embrace pluralities, seeing incongruities as an essential characteristic of contemporary society. Recast within a benign frame of multiple perspectives, contradictions do not have to be reconciled and group-based hierarchies do not have to be examined. Thus, the final syntax of whiteness makes it impossible to recognize structural contradictions grounded in race, class, gender, sexuality, nationality, or specific geographies, and histories of oppression. Stripped of their moorings in structures of domination, contradictions cease to play any role in social transformation. Peaceful coexistence allows contradictory stances to flourish without any recognition that they are rooted in injustice. These syntaxes also highlight the challenges of race whispering. The constant shifting from one racial context to another, even when done skillfully and without obvious difficulty, obscures the authentic positions of a race whisperer. When the language in one context undermines the positions of people you are trying to mobilize in another context, it is hard to determine which beliefs are accurate.

These grammars of whiteness provide particularly useful tools for analyzing central tropes in Barack Obama's most famous discourse on race. Several passages in "A More Perfect Union" replicate the four syntaxes of whiteness at the very moment that Obama intentionally sought to break new ground in U.S. race relations. By placing racial injustice and racism in a previous historical era, Obama invoked the first syntax of whites. He intentionally connected himself to the rhetoric of the civil rights movement, but he did so as someone who sees those grievances as problems that have been resolved through past struggle. It is also worth noting that Obama was reluctant to make this speech; he took up the topic of American racial politics only when it was absolutely unavoidable. In keeping with third-wave sensibilities, he exhibited discomfort about addressing narrow identity categories that prevented him from presenting himself as an individual unbound by race.

First Syntax: Temporality and the Struggles of the Past

In her analysis of third-wave feminist writers, Mane emphasized that homage is paid to anti-racist feminist icons such as Audre Lorde and Gloria Anzaldua, who challenged white privilege and white power. However, this is done in ways that contain anti-racist struggles in the past while discounting the need for contemporary struggle. In a similar fashion, Barack Obama praised leaders of the 1960s civil rights movement and their commitment to legal and policy changes. He celebrated their capacity to change hearts and minds, suggesting that this stage of struggle had ended successfully. Indeed, he cautioned that those who fail to see how much has changed over the past half-century risk misdiagnosing the present. It is within this cautionary frame that Obama addressed the topic of Rev. Jeremiah Wright. He portrayed Jeremiah Wright's criticism of policies regarding racial and cultural imperialism in post–9/11 America as the product of a traumatized subject from America's racial past who cannot grasp contemporary perspectives. He constructed Rev. Wright as mired in the past:

> This is the reality in which Reverend Wright and other African-Americans of his generation grew up. They came of age in the late fifties and early sixties, a time when segregation was still the law of the land and opportunity was systematically constricted.
>
> For the men and women of Reverend Wright's generation, the memories of humiliation and doubt and fear have not gone away; nor have the anger and the bitterness of those years. (Obama 2008b)

In Obama's assessment, Wright's generation suffers from some form of racism PTSD that permanently distorts their views of contemporary society. He suggested that Wright's socialization during the Jim Crow era colors his current views and prevents him from accepting changes in U.S. society. For Wright and his peers, all experiences and critiques of racism and its consequences are ensconced in the past. By implication, reasoned assessments of the current racial landscape that locate and name racism are either misguided accusations by those wedded to the past or incorrect assessments. Political actors who take positions similar to Wright's are viewed as being unable to account for or engage with difference in modern society. When racial injustice is in the past and people who are currently attempting to combat it are relics, Obama leaves little ground for contemporary engagement with ongoing discrimination.

Second Syntax: Events with No History

Mane's second syntax of whiteness involves decontexualization: appropriating claims initially advanced by feminists of color without connecting them to specific historical and geopolitical inequities. Disconnecting the claims from context ignores the impact of specific conditions on marginalized groups. Similarly, Obama makes vague nods to civil rights leaders as his theoretical forebears. He talks about their hard-fought battles for equality, their bravery and sacrifice, and their legacy of struggle. He acknowledges their role in laying the groundwork for his ascent to the nation's highest office. Yet he recounts their efforts as if they were part of a natural unfolding of the U.S. Constitution, an inevitable fulfillment of the founding ideals. He seems to suggest that the civil rights movement is just one more effort by generations of Americans pursuing freedom. However, it is also possible to argue that these same activists enshrined new freedoms in a document that had no intention of including their construction of what it meant to be free. Obama offers,

> And yet words on [the Constitution] would not be enough to deliver slaves from bondage, or provide men and women of every

color and creed their full rights and obligations as citizens of the
United States. What would be needed were Americans in successive generations who were willing to do their part—through protests and struggle, on the streets and in the courts, through a civil
war and civil disobedience and always at great risk—to narrow that
gap between the promise of our ideals and the reality of their time.
(Obama 2008b)

Discussing the Constitution as a document that exemplifies
American ideals of freedom and equality mischaracterizes a historical document that allowed the slave trade to continue until
1808 and calibrated the political worth of those held in bondage
at three-fifths of a person (Smith 1999). Instead of portraying abolitionists and civil rights activists as people who opposed patently
unjust practices embedded in the Constitution, Obama alludes to
temporary deviations from universal ideals. Instead of acknowl-
edging that Black activists crafted an altogether new vision of
equality that differed significantly from the account advanced in
the Declaration of Independence and the Constitution, he depicts
them as participants in a progressive unfolding of "American"
ideals.

As Stephen Marshall (2011) notes, African American leaders
and thinkers "advanced probing critiques of the rhetoric of American elections, mission, and exceptionalism, [yet] sustained rever-
ent attachments and gratitude for the constitutive sacrifice made
by ancestral forebears." African Americans share Obama's respect
for the values of the Constitution, but that respect is strongly tempered by an understanding of the failings of those values. African American leaders have tended to keep both views in play at
all times. Despite the central role the Constitution played in vali-
dating slavery, its "separate but equal" doctrine, and the fiction it

presented of "one person, one vote," in "A More Perfect Union," Obama removed the document from its historical context and portrayed it as an unswerving vehicle for the promotion of equality. Obama aligned himself with this distortion of the historical record, fostering an expectation that African Americans can trust the Constitution to safeguard their rights at a time when Supreme Court decisions might warrant quite a different conclusion.[10] Even more problematic, Obama characterizes the work of civil rights activists and ordinary Black citizens as an outgrowth of American constitutionalism rather than a direct challenge to it.

Third Syntax: All Things Being Equal, Nothing Is Equal

Mane's third syntax of whiteness involves flattening out differences to the point where all experiences of marginalization are deemed equivalent. Within this rhetorical frame, difference produced by patterned and enduring systemic inequalities is indistinguishable from difference produced by individual choice. In its most egregious form, this frame interprets difference that registers profound inequality as congruent to the difference of those who create and exploit inequalities. That is, the identity-based experiences of people of color, which stem from structural policies that generate enduring inequality, are just as valid and important as identities grounded in privilege (e.g., white, male, or heteronormative privilege). In his speech on race, Obama masterfully articulates just such equivalence:

> In fact, a similar anger exists within segments of the white community. Most working- and middle-class white Americans don't feel that they have been particularly privileged by their race. . . . So when they are told to bus their children to a school across town;

when they hear that an African American is getting an advantage in landing a good job or a spot in a good college because of an injustice that they themselves never committed; when they're told that their fears about crime in urban neighborhoods are somehow prejudiced, resentment builds over time. (Obama 2008b)

For Obama, white resentment over policies meant to achieve racial progress and reduce persistent disparities is equated with African American anger in response to four centuries of racial oppression. In his estimation, someone who opposes programs that seek to remedy discrimination (both historical and ongoing) has as much right to be angry as those who are the targets of discrimination. Instead of contesting such a false equivalence, Obama legitimates the comparison.

Fourth Syntax: Irreconcilable Differences

Obama's attempt to legitimate white resentment in response to governmental efforts to redress racial injustice flows rather seamlessly into Mane's final syntax of whiteness: the embrace of irreconcilable contradictions. Instead of engaging "terms that directly contradict one another" (Mane 2012, 86), Obama allows them to coexist without making any effort to reconcile or struggle with contradiction. I have previously argued elsewhere that Obama likens "built-up resentment on the part of whites . . . to black anger at the very discrimination affirmative action is meant to address. At best, these experiences are incongruent. At worst, they are in direct conflict" (Price 2011, 444). By equating radically different sentiments, Obama undermines any effort to have a genuine conversation about racial conflict. By attempting to plot common ground across such radical difference, Obama negates the legitimacy of Black anger in response to continuing injustices. He suggests that Blacks are holding on to past experiences of discrimination too tightly. He tells them to stop being "victims of their past" and "take full responsibility for their own lives." Such admonishments reserved solely for African Americans exempt whites from any responsibility to rectify past racial injustices while reassuring them that racism no longer requires their concern. Incorporating these syntaxes of whiteness, "A More Perfect Union" skews American history and contemporary practice in ways that minimize and occlude racial injustice. As an emblem of the postracial moment, Obama's speech shores up white power and privilege.

Postracialism and the Prospects for Racial Justice

In using Mane's syntaxes of whiteness to interpret Obama's "A More Perfect Union" speech, I don't need to take a stand on Obama's motives. Whether this speech was a strategic intervention to reassure white votes or whether it reflects his "sincere" views of American racial history is not central to my argument. My concern is not with Obama's intentions or his degree of sincerity but with the impact of this historic address. Like many third-wave feminists, Obama advances arguments that explicitly support greater inclusion and cross-race cooperation. Yet his explicit goal may be undone by rhetoric that shores up the white privilege that permeates the fabric of American life (Roediger 2007; McIntosh 1989). Familiar tropes that appeal to equality as a universal value while distorting historical and contemporary contexts unintentionally sustain white privilege.

Operating through third-wave rhetoric, these grammars of whiteness make it difficult to have deeper discussions about the persistence of racism and racial inequality in contemporary life.

Those teachable moments that Obama is fond of mentioning are made more difficult. In the framework of third-wave thought, because everyone's grievances are equal in weight, there is no one entity to hold accountable, no target for blame or justice. To address racism as a contemporary question and to engage in meaningful anti-racist critique requires whites and Blacks to engage in a reflexive process. Yet that reflexive process is truncated by suppositions about postracialism and the "end of racism." Postracial notions are often bolstered by the circulation of "race-neutral" language, but this language often masks the fact that race-specific targeting continues in many policies. Without a discussion of systemic white privilege, conversations about race can lead to no good ends for African Americans.

Addressing contemporary racism requires critical analysis of existing policies from the standpoint of people who are not privileged by them. Instead of encomiums to hard work and the benefits conferred by the American system, there must be sustained attention to the disparate impact of policies, particularly with respect to those who bear the weight of intersecting disadvantages grounded in race, class, ethnicity, gender, sexuality, and undocumented status. The grammars of whiteness ignore evidence of continuing inequities and impact not only those who are often caricatured as racist (such as Republicans, southerners, or poor whites) but also self-proclaimed progressives. The grammar outlined here is not the language of the right; it is the language of the left, whose members view themselves as better managers of diversity issues. They must call on themselves to account for how even their ways of explaining the world may uphold the very structures they claim to oppose. Challenging the discursive power of the syntaxes of whiteness requires narrative shifts for people who view themselves as already critically engaging the diverse world, such as liberals, feminists, and third-wavers. Such a discursive challenge would necessarily unsettle existing beliefs on the part of these groups about authority and trust, especially as they are reinforced by popular media sources. Just as Rev. Wright was taken out of context and his words subjected to distortion by conservative activists, the media, and (to a lesser extent) Barack Obama, opinion leaders of many stripes routinely use the grammars of whiteness to undermine evidence of racial injustice.

Syntaxes of whiteness make it more difficult to demonstrate that material inequalities are produced by structural injustice. When racism is permanently relegated to the past, alternative explanations of inequality must come from other sources. Cultural pathology becomes a default justification for persistent inequality (Steinberg 1995). Insistence that racism has been overcome also creates a division between "old" and "new" Blacks. Activists and scholars who offer a cogent critique of U.S. society and its policies and advance claims about contemporary racism are viewed as individuals who are tethered to the past, who are unable to cope, and, ultimately, who are irrelevant. Their views are rendered fertile targets for derision and mocked as altogether "out of step" with the times. When individuals or groups who have been negatively affected by racism speak out about discrimination and oppression, "new" voices within Black communities denounce these claims as illegitimate. A side effect of these intraracial divisions is that whites no longer need to devote efforts to debunk claims concerning racial injustice; they can simply repeat the words of "new" Blacks.

In this postracial era, what constitutes racism or sexism is debated within a framework that posits all perspectives as equal. When all claims are deemed equally valid, it is near-impossible to demarcate a racist incident. When all ideas are accorded equal respect, all claims of victimization are validated, and all sentiments of anger and resentment are deemed righteous, racist episodes become unidentifiable. They are replaced by "teachable moments" with no real lesson plans and no possibility of conclusive resolution.

4

An Officer and Two Gentlemen

The Great Beer Summit of 2009

In other chapters, I have focused primarily on rhetoric that is well honed and scripted. This chapter examines the infamous "Beer Summit" between President Obama, Harvard professor Henry Louis Gates, and Officer James Crowley in the White House Rose Garden after a tense incident in Cambridge, Massachusetts. This incident was a watershed moment for how race would be dealt with in the Obama administration. According to the Pew Research Center's Journalism Project, Gates's arrest was the "largest single event explicitly tied to race in the way it was covered during the year" (Guskin, Khan, and Mitchell 2010, 2) and accounted for the largest share of stories about African Americans on talk radio, online news, and cable news. There is no doubt that the series of events following Gates's arrest were instructive for how Obama might handle racial disagreements as the first Black president.

At its most basic level, this is really a story about a test of wills between Gates and Crowley that is undergirded by historic and subconscious assumptions about race and belonging. Gates's race suggested to Crowley that he did not belong in the upscale area of Cambridge where the confrontation took place and the professor resided. It is a familiar tale that was animated by the presence of the most distinguished African American scholar in the United States and possibly the world. Gates was also the host and producer of a series of PBS specials about African American history and genealogy as well as

editor-in-chief of the popular news website *The Root*. More significantly, Gates was President Obama's good friend and enthusiastic
supporter. As a result, the incident received widespread coverage
and discussion and ultimately made its way to a White House press
conference. The focus here is less on the actual incident, which
was eventually quickly and quietly settled, than on the political
melodrama that followed President Obama's statements at the
press conference. What surely seemed to Obama to be a statement
of support for a friend who was a senior citizen, walked with a
cane, and charged with trespassing and disorderly conduct on his
own porch became a political football that was interpreted, reinterpreted, and misinterpreted by friends and foes alike for talking
points, ratings, and political gamesmanship.

The Incident: Law and Order?

On July 16, 2009, Harvard University professor Henry Louis Gates
Jr. was returning to his Cambridge, Massachusetts, home from a
trip to China. After having trouble with the front door, he asked
his taxi driver to come and help him pry the door open. As they
were struggling with the door, a witness dialed 911 to report the
incident. The witness told the dispatcher that she observed two
men who seemed to be trying to pry the door open of a private
home. The transcript of the witness's call suggests that she was not
sure that this was a burglary and offered an alternative interpretation of the events, "that perhaps a resident was simply struggling to
open his own door" (Ogletree 2012). By all reports, when the Cambridge police officer arrived, Professor Gates was already inside his
home and was quite aggravated by the arrival of the police and the
suggestion that he might not belong in his own home. When the
officer on the scene, Sgt. James Crowley, entered Gates's residence,

Gates showed the officer his Harvard ID card and his driver's license, both of which corroborated the fact that he was indeed in his own home.

Reports differ about what happened as the situation began to escalate. Harvard Law professor Charles Ogletree (2012) sums up the scenario: "Neither of these men knew each other, and so presumptions ruled the progression of events, neither felt respected by the other and neither trusted each other." Gates and Crowley began to argue back and forth. Sgt. Crowley called more Cambridge Police Department cars to the scene and the Harvard University Police Department, and another officer entered Gates's residence as the scene became more heated. Professor Gates said the problem started when Sgt. Crowley refused to give his name and badge number. Crowley says he gave him the number multiple times but Gates was yelling over him and didn't hear. At some point, Sgt. Crowley left the residence and told Professor Gates that if he wanted to continue to talk he had come out onto the porch. More arguing ensued as Gates followed Crowley and the other officer onto the porch. The commotion attracted some onlookers and more cops arrived at the scene. In the end, Professor Gates was arrested for causing a public commotion at his own home. He was handcuffed, fingerprinted, photographed, and held at the Cambridge police station. Because of Gates's prominence, the arrest was picked up by the media and began to reverberate around the nation. Professor Gates and his surrogates were interviewed about the incident and his mug shot was widely distributed.

After standing by Officer Crowley's decision to arrest Gates and denying the impact of race in the events, the Cambridge police department dropped the charges against Professor Gates five days later. Robert Siegel of *All Things Considered* noted that "police in Cambridge, Massachusetts, now are calling the arrest unfortunate.

Gates and his allies are calling it racism." At the time of his arrest Professor Gates was 58 years old and walked with the assistance of a cane. During the handcuffing process, Gates pointed out that he would not be able to navigate the stairs with his hands cuffed behind his back. Officer Crowley then cuffed his hands in front of him and went back inside the house to retrieve Gates's cane (Ogletree 2012). This was hardly the description of someone who presented a major threat to the officers, and the arrest occurred after it was already established that Gates was not, in fact, a burglar. Initially the eyewitness did not say the men she saw (ostensibly Gates and his driver) were African American and provided a racial description only after being asked about the issue by the emergency dispatcher (Ogletree 2012). Shortly after the incident, one commentator on NPR noted that "disorderly conduct cases are jokingly referred to by police as, quote, 'contempt of cop charges,' meaning . . . the person arrested insulted the officers, but often didn't really break the law" (Arnold 2009). Though the actual incident was primarily settled in less than a week, the insertion of President Obama's evaluation of what happened opened up a larger debate about race and policing; whether the president was anti-cop and pro-Black—two positions that were framed as oppositional; and what it all meant for his burgeoning presidency.

Gates's arrest and the subsequent reaction of the public provided America with what President Obama likes to call a "teachable moment." He uses this language often around multicultural misunderstandings. For him, these are times for the American people to pause, listen to opposing views on a particular topic, and potentially meet in a new space of tolerance and mutual understanding. This chapter will show that, paradoxically, the important lessons learned here were those the president learned—about when and how he could talk about racially contentious issues. He learned that he would have to be prepared and measured in all reactions to questions regarding race, especially questions dealing specifically with the African American community. When Obama didn't do so in the case of Gates, many whites, regardless of party affiliation, turned against him for taking a clear side. This was true despite the fact that most conservatives and libertarians would clearly see arresting a man on his own front porch as a violation of rights. If race and Obama were not a part of the equation, a story like this would be an example of government intrusion into the lives of American citizens that conservatives consistently use as political fodder. While Obama's opponents and right-wing political commentators rushed to disagree with his views about the Gates affair, many support the right of homeowners to use guns to protect themselves in their own home. Interestingly, when Obama took a similar position (minus the guns) in support of Professor Gates, there was no common ground.

This incident was the first time Obama addressed race explicitly as president. There was no precedent for what happened, no sense of how Americans would receive having a Black president talk about race on national television. No one knew how the first Black president would frame a racial issue that Blacks and whites saw very differently. Would he take the position previous presidents had taken by focusing the role of president as commander-in-chief and endorse the actions of law enforcement personnel? Or would he take the side of the African American community, which has had long-standing grievances with the policing strategies law enforcement agencies use? The Gates incident became the first visible test case of race relations in what was popularly seen as the dawn of a postracial epoch.

The perspectives of Blacks and whites on policing tend to be quite divergent. African Americans have less confidence in the police than whites do. Recent studies have shown that only 10 percent of African Americans "believe minorities receive equal treatment with whites in the criminal justice system," and only 20 percent believe that cops treat all races equally (Balz and Clement 2014). More than half of all whites believe that all races receive equal treatment from the police and the criminal justice system (Balz and Clement 2014). Blacks are also more than twice as likely as whites to believe that high Black male incarceration rates are due to discrimination. In addition, Blacks are less likely to believe that police are ethical and honest and more likely to believe that new civil rights laws are needed (Newport 2014). How President Obama responded to a nationally covered case that dealt with on-going differences in the way Blacks and whites see and experience American law enforcement could only serve to signal what public discourse on race would look like going forward. A great deal of emotional and political weight was put on the shoulders of the first Black president in a nation that continues to be racially balkanized. More so than the presidents before him, all of whom were white, President Obama needed to demonstrate fairness and objectivity. Candidate Obama's strategy was to emphasize universal messages that cut across racial divides rather than exacerbate them, hence President Obama was well aware of the need to be very cautious about racial issues.

The Gates controversy took place when Obama had been in office for seven months and Obama was still trying to leverage his historic win to get his policy priorities implemented. The president was asked about it as a last question in a long exchange with reporters that was preceded by a lengthy speech in a primetime press conference about health care. The issue arose in the fifty-first minute of a televised event that lasted fifty-four minutes. It seemed fairly clear that the president had not really considered what he planned to say or how it might be received by the public. Obama's answer to the question about Gates thus also represents a rare instance of the president offering unprepared remarks, particularly about race. I mention spontaneity because I think it plays an important role in the escalation of the situation. Being asked about an ongoing police investigation involving a friend is tricky for anyone to deal with. When speaking with the largest and most powerful microphone in the world, whatever you say about it will impact not just the particulars of the case but will have a far-reaching impact on various constituencies within the American electorate, such as racial advocacy groups, police unions, and political opponents. In this context, the president was unlikely to offer his usual nuanced answer that provided a common starting point for a larger discussion.

It is also interesting to note that the reporter asking the question was Lynn Sweet of the *Chicago Sun-Times*. Because she was a seasoned reporter from Obama's hometown, she had observed him longer and likely knew him better than any other reporter in the room. Though she has been accused by the right of being biased in favor of the president, she was one of the few reporters who continuously reported instances of Obama using Black pathology narratives when he spoke to large Black crowds. Her familiarity with the ins and outs of the Obama campaign's inner circle and the fact that she was attuned to the racial specifics of the new presidency helped explain her knowledge of both Gates's arrest and its connection to the president. In an interview later, Sweet said she was prepared to ask a different question about the health care debate but because so much had been covered on that topic, she decided to go a different way (McGowan 2009). As a result of the brief exchange with Lynn Sweet, the president was forced to spend more than a week and a considerable amount of political energy walking back his statements. That retraction shaped how Obama would deal publicly with racially charged issues for the rest of his presidency. Any future statements about race would be planned and vetted and would focus on diplomatic rhetoric.

The consequence of the president's remarks was that attention was redirected from his most important policy priority at the time—health care—to a focus on Gates's arrest and Obama's beliefs about whites. Obama himself noted the distraction: "Over the last two days as we've discussed this [arrest] issue, I don't know if you've noticed, but nobody has been paying much attention to health care" (quoted in J. Walsh 2009). The discussion of the Gates affair lasted no more than a week or two, but the damage was profound. Health care reform was supposed to be Obama's signature piece of legislation in his first term. Getting Americans to sign on for universal health care and the government's role in facilitating it was going to be a hard task. Newspaper editor Don Wycliff (2009) noted that "Obama was going to need every ounce of public support he could muster to achieve even modest health care reform. The sad fact is that the Gates-Crowley distraction has deprived him of a measurable degree of support." There can be no doubt that when attention turned back to health care reform, the president had lost some footing. A spontaneous insertion of a racial issue had diminished the political latitude of President Obama.

The Press Conference: What about Skip?

The president situated his answer to Sweet's question in a larger discussion about racial profiling that he, like all Blacks, has experienced. He offered a lengthy answer that identified Professor Gates as a personal friend and admitted that he was not totally clear on the details. If he had stopped there, nothing contentious would have come from his response. His decision to go into detail about the case without a briefing led to a storm of controversy. Here is a partial offering of what he said, which includes the most controversial statements:

> The police officer comes in, I'm sure there's some exchange of words, but my understanding is, is that Professor Gates then shows his ID to show that this is his house. And at that point, he gets arrested for disorderly conduct—charges which are later dropped.
>
> Now, I don't know, not having been there and not seeing all the facts, what role race played in that, but I think it's fair to say, number one, any of us would be pretty angry; number two, *that the Cambridge Police acted stupidly in arresting somebody when there was already proof that they were in their own home*; and number three, what I think we know separate and apart from this incident is that there is a long history in this country of African Americans and Latinos being stopped by law enforcement disproportionately. That's just a fact. (Obama 2009b; italics added)

In subsequent days, the media and Obama's political opponents seized upon the word "stupidly." They questioned whether his words were too harsh and were outside of the realm of presidential behavior (Simon 2009; Van Susteren 2009). There were questions about whether he should have spoken about a local matter from the president's podium, thus muddying any investigations (Simon 2009; Robbins 2009; O'Brien et al. 2009). Significant debate centered on whose side he seemed to be taking—that of Blacks or that of the cops (NBC News 2009; MacDonald 2009). The decision to take a side at all was questioned (Wallsten, Nicholas, and Simon 2009). Most of all, every conversation was held under the hyper-focused lens of race and race relations within the context of how the first Black president would govern.

The president's comments were immediately seen as offensive by policing organizations throughout the country. Massachusetts police unions demanded an apology in a press conference at which a Black police officer, who was present at the scene, Leon Lashley, denied the impact of race in the event (Salsberg and Lavoie 2009). Police officers around the country took the president's statement personally. One Boston police officer sent an e-mail to co-workers referring to Gates as "a banana-eating jungle monkey" (Mansbridge 2009). In addition, a significant amount of misinformation was disseminated about what had actually happened. Reports of the conversation between the 911 dispatcher and the witness who called the incident in differed greatly about whether or not she told the dispatcher that the men were breaking into the home and whether she mentioned they were Black. Later it was revealed that the witness never said they were Black (Kates 2009). She informed the dispatcher that she only saw the men's backs and when prompted by the dispatcher said she thought one might be Hispanic (Lindsay 2009). Despite that, she was criticized and felt compelled to use the news media to ask for people to stop calling her a racist (Lindsay 2009). Within a few days of his initial answer, President Obama was apologizing for not "calibrating" his words more carefully. Obama explained,

> I unfortunately gave an impression that I was maligning the Cambridge police department or Sgt. Crowley specifically. I could have calibrated those words differently. (quoted in Johns and Lemon 2009)

He came short of apologizing for what he said by focusing on his intent, which had not been to insult the Cambridge police or Sgt.

Crowley.[1] President Obama then dutifully reached out to Gates, Crowley, and other parties involved. Ultimately those discussions led to the beer summit.

Obama's attempt to clarify his comments at the press conference seemed generally unsatisfactory to all sides. People who had supported his defense of Professor Gates felt that Obama's later statements and actions undercut the power of the initial defense (O'Brien et al. 2009). The decision to call Crowley and apologize to him personally suggested not just that Gates's behavior was questionable but that complaints by African Americans about police overreach more broadly might also be up for debate. In addition, some felt that by attempting to take back his critique, he undermined the claims he had made and that this was a missed opportunity to deal with racial profiling. In a telling discussion by panelists on CNN's program *The Situation Room*, reporter Soledad O'Brien mentioned that attendees at the recent annual meeting of the Urban League felt that "he didn't use the opportunity to have a real discussion about race" (O'Brien et al. 2009). In contrast, opponents of Obama's sentiments felt he had not gone far enough and should have recanted his statements completely. For them, anything short of an apology would be hollow, and even an apology would only stop the damage, not repair the breach it had created. Noted Black conservative Larry Elder expressed this viewpoint:

> I would be flattered that the president invited me to the White House, but I would respectfully say, until and unless you directly apologize to me and my department for accusing me falsely of racially profiling Professor Gates, I refuse the invitation. (O'Brien et al. 2009)

During the height of the coverage, the only real common ground between the two camps was dissatisfaction with Obama. Hence, although the beer summit garnered an enormous amount of attention, it was unlikely to change the views of the American people on race in any substantial way.

The Beer Summit

Two weeks after Gates's arrest, Gates and Crowley came to the White House with their families to meet with each other under the watchful gaze of the international media and millions of Americans watching cable news. Each family was given a special tour of the White House, although Gates had visited previously. After their family visits, President Obama, Professor Gates, and Officer Crowley retreated to the Rose Garden along with Vice President Joe Biden to have a beer. The men casually strolled outside with their shirt sleeves rolled up and offered lots of smiles. However, like most things related to this new and historic presidential administration, every detail of the event emerged as discussion points. There were discussions about what it meant that these men were having a beer and not wine or hard liquor. NPR's Liz Halloran (2009) interviewed brewers from around the country about what it meant for the men to share a beer instead of a "Washington state pinot noir or a summery gin and tonic." This was after questions about whether the men were required to drink American brews and after avid beer drinkers queried the meanings of the different choices. A Vermont television station reported that local brewers were upset because all the men chose beers that were not made by American companies, despite the fact that President Obama chose Bud Light, an iconic American beer (the brand had been acquired by a foreign firm) (Tomisho and Williamson 2009). The brewers released a statement expressing their "chagrin" that none of the beers consumed at the summit were made by American-owned companies (WPTZ.com 2009). Members of the media also commented about the fact that they were not allowed to listen in on the conversation. They were forced to glean the tone of the conversation through the lenses of their cameras along with the rest of the American people.

In a post-event press conference, all the men were very clear that the conversation had been "friendly and thoughtful" and that Professor Gates and Sgt. Crowley would meet to talk alone at a later date (Mansbridge 2009). Both men left the meeting more aware of each other's positions but relatively unchanged. A Fox News reporter noted that the "two gentlemen . . . agreed to disagree on a particular issue"—presumably, the incidents surrounding Gates's arrest (Van Susteren 2009). Officer Crowley mentioned that he had hand delivered a letter to President Obama from an African American officer in the Cambridge Police Department, Leon Lashley. The note discussed the fact that many people were starting to label him an "Uncle Tom" for supporting his fellow officer. He also told the president that he thought Professor Gates's actions "may have caused grave and potentially irreparable harm to the struggle for racial harmony in the country and throughout the world" (O'Brien et al. 2009). All of the attendees reported that the event went off without a hitch, but clearly there was tension underlying their civil demeanor (Cooper and Goodnough 2009).

Outside the White House lawn, though, the discussion was still in full swing and the level of vitriol was growing. The discourse around Obama's comments and the beer summit quickly became a litmus test of American race relations in a way that Gates's actual arrest had not been. What did the president's comments tell everyone about his racial beliefs? Had something been missed during the campaign that suggested a more complicated inner life that included anti-law enforcement and anti-white sentiments? In the next section, I look at the discussions on cable news and talk radio in the aftermath of these events in an effort to understand how Obama's future responses to racial issues were informed by this moment.

The Aftermath

Like views about the relationship between law enforcement and African Americans, the response to the Gates incident was divided along racial lines. Blacks largely supported Obama's initial position, and whites took issue with what the president said. The incident tapped into a fairly consistent racial fault line that revealed the deep chasms between Blacks and whites on a multitude of issues, particularly policing and law enforcement. An NBC News/Wall Street Journal poll taken two weeks after the initial incident found, "by a 27%–11% margin, Americans say that Harvard professor Henry Louis Gates Jr. was more at fault for his recent arrest . . . But a greater number, 29%, believe that both were equally at fault. And 31% say they didn't know enough to have an opinion" (Murray 2009). Whites were eight times more likely than Blacks to say that Gates was more at fault and Blacks were five times more likely to say that Crowley was at fault (Davis 2009). Don Wycliff (2009) put it more bluntly, "The truth is, Obama has been 'on probation' with a substantial number of whites, who were willing to take a chance on and tolerate him as long as he didn't act black. When he violated that condition with his remarks on Gates-Crowley, those people yanked his probation." The meaning individuals attach to the Gates incident was heavily dependent upon the observer's race, and the space between how racial groups see Obama's response was wide.

These kinds of stark disagreements between racial groups have come to be expected when contentious issues become front-page news and media fodder. What was more intriguing about public opinion during that period was both the level of attention paid to the story and the disproportionate reaction of Obama's opponents. There were few moderate responses: clearer heads would not prevail. Instead, Fox News hosts and conservative radio pundits claimed that Obama's defense of a friend who ultimately had the charges dropped against him was a window into a deep and seething anti-white view that Obama secretly held (O'Reilly, Crowley, and Colmes 2009; Beck 2009; Huff 2009). Obama's opponents saw in his off-the-cuff response to Lynn Sweet's question at the White House press conference the Obama who was a member of Jeremiah Wright's church, where anti-white and anti-American opinions were purportedly meted out in every other sentence. Here was the first inkling of the angry Black man Obama's opponents had been looking for, and they used this moment to point this out to their listeners and viewers.

There is a movie from the Blaxploitation era called *The Spook Who Sat by the Door*, which was based on a novel written by Sam Greenlee (1973), who also directed the film. As an underground favorite of Blaxploitation fans for many years, the film has recently been re-released to a younger and wider audience. *The Spook* tells the story of Dan Freeman, the first African American to integrate the Central Intelligence Agency (CIA), despite the agency's best efforts to prevent him from making it through the requisite training. Freeman succeeds, unlike the African American men who did not complete the training, because he is conservative, studious, and excellent at all tasks, but also because he is quite conciliatory. In other words, he goes along to get along and causes no trouble. When Freeman leaves the CIA, however, he uses the skills he has acquired to transform a Chicago street gang into guerrilla freedom fighters. Because of his affiliation with the CIA and the fact that he has played the part of the company man so well, even his closest friends are surprised to learn that he is behind the civil unrest that erupts into rioting and then complete urban warfare. The premise of the movie is obviously fantastical, but it is instructive here on two levels. First, many people are a fan of this movie because it upends the notion of the Uncle Tom by creating a character who is able to convince whites he is their ally, while simultaneously dismantling the system that heavily constrains Black life. Imagine Cecil Gaines from *The Butler* being a secret revolutionary who uses information gleaned while serving coffee at the White House to plan an attack on the American government.[2] The film plays on the notion that outside of the white gaze Blacks take on not just a different personality but also very different social and political positions that are decidedly anti-white. It is a Black Power–era version of the traditional Brer Rabbit tale in which the underdog bests the people who have underestimated his intelligence and overestimated their own. James Scott (1992) places these kinds of turnaround tales in the realm of the hidden transcript where less powerful members of society are able to create a space of empowerment. For whites who have the cultural knowledge to read the film's message from the perspective of Blacks, the film offers a nightmare scenario. A by-product of power is that the people who perform menial functions fade into the scenery. They move through the same spaces as the powerful, but they do so quietly with as little intrusion as possible. The insinuation that the powerless are gathering information about the vulnerabilities of the powerful foregrounds the powerless and makes the spaces more dangerous and fraught for everyone present.

Barack Obama is no Dan Freeman. I mention this film to suggest an ongoing concern of some whites that Blacks have an inner life that whites cannot access and the fear that this inner life is especially hostile to whites. It is a belief that, because of the long history of racial injustice and animosity, there are some parts of the Black community whites cannot apprehend. In this framework, the Barack Obama who presents his views as measured and balanced about racial issues becomes a potential trickster like Brer Rabbit or others depicted in African American folktales dating back to slavery—those who "flout the norms of society, using cunning, humor, and deceit to obtain personal gain" (Smith 2005, 179). The key to the trickster narrative is that they are often perceived as weak in some way and are thus able to use the fact that they are underestimated to outwit and ultimately best their more powerful opponent (Roberts 1990). Lawrence Levine (2007) argues that these trickster tales convey important messages about morality, the nature of power, and the possibility of future victories. *The Spook Who Sat by the Door* is a modern trickster tale in which Dan Freeman is a hero to African Americans who catches the whites in the film off guard because they have underestimated his intellect and bought into his pretense that he is one of them. Dan Freeman's agenda is not revealed until it is too late and all hell has broken loose.

In the weeks after the Gates incident, commentators talked about Obama as if he had been exposed as a Dan Freeman. The comments he made at the press conference offered a glimpse into Obama's judgment and views on race, and some believed that his remarks confirmed their suspicions during the general elections that President Obama was angry and unpatriotic and as a result was unfit to lead. Some Obama critics believed that his remarks at the press conference revealed the same views that were hinted at by his association with Jeremiah Wright and other "Chicago radicals." These critics believed that despite the fact that they had warned the American public, Barack Obama was elected president and that his reaction to Henry Louis Gates had proved them right (Politico. com 2009; Limbaugh 2009; K. Walsh 2009). Conservative media pundits and commentators seized upon this moment to suggest that a spontaneous comment about a close friend's unfortunate arrest represented an underlying hostility. For instance, Rush Limbaugh believed that "the president's reaction was not presidential," concluding that there are only two types of reactions from Blacks: "we got the militant black reaction, we got the Cornel West angry reaction" (Guskin, Khan, and Mitchell 2010). In the view of Limbaugh and other critics, the target of Obama's latent ire was white people. Critics also claimed that Obama's failure to investigate the incident thoroughly before taking a public position was a sign that his temperament was poorly matched for a job as important and as difficult as the American presidency (Simon 2009; Van Susteren 2009).

The first aspect of conservative coverage surrounding this event focused heavily on demonstrating that Gates had not been racially profiled and that consequently, the president had unnecessarily and maliciously played the race card. Noted scholar Shelby Steele (2008) suggests that belying "Mr. Obama's 'post-racialism' was a promise to operate outside of tired cultural narratives. But he has a demon arm of reflexive racialism—identity politics, Rev. Jeremiah Wright, and now Skip Gates." Those who were in this camp argued that the president's decision to insert race into the discussion muddied the waters and mischaracterized the facts. Their assertion was facilitated by the president's own admission that he did not know all the facts of the case.

Reframing the story of the arrest as one of a cop who was simply doing his job and an elite professor who believed he was overly entitled is an attempt to render race irrelevant and substitute a class argument instead. Bill O'Reilly called Gates "a well-known far-left professor who's got a chip on his shoulder" (O'Reilly, Crowley, and Colmes 2009). According to Thomas Frank (2009), "commentators on the right zeroed in on the fact that Mr. Gates is an 'Ivy League big shot,' a 'limousine liberal,' and a star professor at Harvard, an institution they regard with special loathing." Interestingly, one of the critiques of Obama during the 2008 campaign was that he was too professorial and, as Jack Stripling (2010) of the *Chronicle of Higher Education* has noted, "if the term 'professor' is used in politics, it is seldom a compliment." It refers to a tendency toward liberal beliefs but also to intellectual and class snobbery that is most exemplified in the way professors are perceived to be aloof and condescending to people who are less educated (Stripling 2010). In the mind of conservative pundits, Obama and Gates had transgressed both their racial and class limits. Thus, a class status that was advantageous to two African Americans appeared to complicate this story. Rush Limbaugh referred to Professor Gates, whose nickname is Skip, as "Skippy Gates" as he described him to his listeners (Limbaugh 2009).[3] The diminution of a name that is already a nickname seemed both deliberate and intended to offend Gates and his supporters, including the president.

As a complement to painting Gates as the angry aggressor, conservatives also mentioned Sgt. Crowley's experience teaching seminars on how to avoid racial profiling. To many white conservatives, this fact alone eliminated the possibility that race could have been a factor in the arrest. In this logic, Crowley was an expert about how *not* to profile and thus could not have profiled anyone, especially Professor Gates (quoted in Simon 2009). NPR host Scott Simon, paired the story that Crowley taught classes about avoiding racial profiling with the little-known fact that Crowley had been on the scene and had tried to save the life of African American NBA all-star and Boston Celtics starter Reggie Lewis when he collapsed at Brandeis. (Lewis eventually died.) It was unclear how the latter story informed the context of Gates's arrest, but the implication seemed to be that knowing about the Lewis incident diminished the chances that Crowley was a racist. It presented Crowley as a person who was actively working to keep Blacks in his community safe.

Once the discussion was reframed with Gates as the aggressor, and Crowley was insulated from claims of racism, conservatives turned their attention to whether or not the president had shown poor judgment and poor leadership by interfering in an ongoing investigation. Questions about his judgment at the press conference led to concerns about his judgment generally. According to his critics, it was inappropriate for a president to interfere with local matters no matter what the issue was. Juan Williams, then of NPR, summarized the problem conservatives had regarding Obama:

> President Obama has tremendous appeal, and much of it is tied to his image as a racially healing force in American society, given our history. And this week, he seemed all to at ease with lobbing presidentially powered words in what was a local fracas, and did so without the facts. (quoted in Simon 2009)

Presidents are responsible for an entire country and locally elected officials are responsible for smaller jurisdictions. In the minds of conservatives, President Obama had violated clearly demarcated boundaries between federal and local governments. By not understanding that and not showing personal restraint, he manifested their belief that he was unprepared for such an important job.

Commentators characterized Obama as having "hair trigger judgment" (Van Susteren 2009). They claimed that he lacked the self-control necessary to be America's national representative (Van Susteren 2009). Though George Stephanopoulos, a former Clinton administration official and the host of ABC's *Good Morning America*, didn't believe the incident would damage the president in the long run, he said it appeared as if President Obama "felt like the press conference was over" when he answered the Lynn Sweet's question (Tapper 2009). This was particularly problematic, according to Stephanopoulos, because the White House staff should have known the question was coming and should have prepared the president better. Critics on the right were far less forgiving. Fox News contributor Dick Morris explained:

> The problem I have is with the president of the United States. This guy who has his finger on the button, *who on his judgment can destroy the world* simply by pushing a button or flipping a switch, needs to tell the American people about his conduct, not the cop's and the professor's." (quoted in Van Susteren 2009; italics added)

Such critiques suggested a bigger question: If Obama failed on such a small test in the beginning of his presidency, what would this mean for bigger challenges such as health care reform?

Some critics of Obama's handling of the Gates/Crowley affair accused the president of harboring hostility toward whites. No one pushed this argument more than Fox News host Glenn Beck, who appeared on multiple shows on the Fox News network during this period to discuss his belief that Obama didn't just lack discernment; he was, in fact, a racist (Politico.com 2009). In Beck's assessment, President Obama's criticism of an officer who arrested a man for being irate about being treated like a criminal in his own home amounted to an obvious sign that the president did not like white people. Beck summarized his argument: "This president, I think, has exposed himself as a guy, *over and over and over again,* who has a deep-seated hatred for white people or white culture" (Politico.com 2009; italics added). Beck expressed these views on the Fox News morning show *Fox and Friends* with virtually no pushback on July 28, 2009. Another reporter responded by asking where were "Obama's white advisors" who could help him with this. Later in this same program, Beck reiterated his belief in an oddly contradictory statement. He hedged a bit, then returned to his initial accusation: "I'm not saying he doesn't like white people. I'm saying he has a problem. He has a—this guy is, I believe, a racist" (quoted in Politico.com 2009). Beck's views represent the most extreme critique of Obama, but it is difficult to call him an outlier; he was by no means a marginal figure from a marginal news outpost. He was a featured member of the primetime lineup of a popular news channel who boldly called the sitting president of the United States (and the nation's first African American president) a racist.[4]

Within days, Gates and the city of Cambridge attempted to put the incident behind them, but this proved to be impossible because of the scrutiny of the national media the president's comments had sparked. Racial conversations have a tendency to quickly balkanize. *Salon.com* contributor Joan Walsh (2009), in her discussion of why she did not believe the beer summit would be effective, highlighted the fact that "many people seemed to be watching [the beer summit] from behind their own racial barricades." Given the history of race in America, these barricades are more like giant reinforced steel walls. In the end, the attention paid to this issue dissipated. The country essentially learned nothing new from this first "teachable moment" of the Obama administration. However, Barack Obama and interested observers potentially learned an enormous amount about the difficulties of navigating racial issues during his presidency. After this experience, the president did not deal overtly with racial issues again until his second term, which suggests that he intentionally steered clear of the discussion, not that the need for the discussion ceased. It was not until the death of Trayvon Martin and the acquittal of his killer that Obama spoke directly about race from the White House podium again. On that day, July 9, 2013, he spoke about race during a nationally televised press conference not as a part of a commemoration of history or a moment to celebrate a national achievement but as an opportunity to have a sober conversation about the disparate impact of race on Black Americans.

It was clear that for many Americans what constituted an appropriate racial issue that the president should discuss was confined to a narrow set of questions and that Professor Gates's arrest was not one of them. The incident also pushed some to argue against their own ideological position in an effort to maintain an oppositional position vis-à-vis the president. Private property rights and the protection of those rights is a cornerstone of modern American conservatism. When Professor Gates was arrested, conservatives were already making arguments that the government was reaching beyond the limits of its power in order to oppose everything from President Obama's health care reform efforts to the First Lady's more modest attempts to get children to exercise more. The Obamas were accused of attempting to create a "nanny state" that imposed government control and regulation on every aspect of American life (Hamby 2008; Kristol 2008; Carney 2012).[5] Conservatives could have used the arrest of Professor Gates in his own home to illustrate the concerns they were having about administration policies. Surely private citizens had a right to maintain the integrity of their own home and not be encroached upon by the government. Instead, President Obama's and Professor Gates's race created a context in which the role of Blacks' interactions with law enforcement agents and agencies could not be ignored. The mere fact that the president brought up the role of race meant that his political opponents could not maintain their commitment to conservative principles and to opposing the president.

The vitriol that emerged after the president defended Professor Gates and other Black men who have experienced racial profiling also revealed the limits of Obama's ability to talk about African American issues—outside of his tendency to make more universal arguments that included African Americans among the multiple groups who might potentially benefit from his policy proposals. In the aftermath of the Gates affair, there were three ways the president could safely talk about race without major criticism. First, he could stress the common experiences that unify citizens regardless of their racial origin. He began his life on the national political stage at the 2004 Democratic National Convention with this argument. He laid out his own multiracial heritage as evidence of American exceptionalism and continued to reiterate that point. Like the president, Professor Gates had a trailblazing career as an Ivy League professor and TV host. Gates's story could just as easily demonstrate the president's arguments of American exceptionalism. Second, he could tell racial stories that blurred or obscured past racial conflicts. He could tell stories about how the civil rights movement was not just about changing laws and the minds of whites but about the work that Black people need to do on themselves as well, as he had done in Selma in 2007 (Obama 2007). Finally, he could tell racial stories that reinforced beliefs about inherent Black pathology, as he had already done on many occasions, including the fiftieth anniversary of the 1963 March on Washington (Obama 2013b). What he could not do was defend the rights of Black people not to be profiled by police or their white neighbors. Doing that gave conservatives the ammunition to call into question both his judgment and his fitness for the presidency and his feelings toward all whites.

Unsurprisingly, he did not discuss race again on national media until four years later and well into his second term, when he discussed the outcome of the trial of the man who killed Trayvon Martin. Martin was followed and killed by a local resident of his condominium complex in Sanford, Florida, while he was returning home from a convenience store. George Zimmerman, Martin's killer, a self-appointed member of the local Neighborhood Watch, was found not guilty of murder. After the not-guilty verdict, the president held a moving press conference at which he discussed the impact of the verdict on the Black community. This time he waited until the trial was complete and a verdict had been reached before he commented and was careful to indicate that he had waited because he didn't want to interfere with the local process.

President Obama's response to the Gates incident is one of his least successful engagements with race in his national political career. Success, in this case, would be defined as the absence of a firestorm in response to his comments in a way that distracts from his policy goals. His goal was to place the arrest of his friend into a larger conversation about racial profiling and the continuing challenge of persistent inequality. There was no reason to believe that the nation would oppose this kind of discussion. The election of an African American president surely signaled an opening in the nation's long-standing racial impasse. However, the arrest of Henry Louis Gates Jr. demonstrated that race in the age of Obama was more complicated. Barack Obama's election, ironically, seemed to forestall these kinds of conversations. The heated debate and intense criticism that followed Obama's remarks about the Gates incident also demonstrated that one of the major benefits of having an African American president—that is, having someone who could articulate racial group concerns on a larger scale—would not be realized any time soon. If any mention of specifically Black experiences and preferences from the nation's highest office set off such a firestorm, then it would be too politically costly to do so.

Black Men and the Cops

It also seems important in the current context that the president's first and least effective statement on race relations was about a Black man's interaction with the police. It resonates even more given the fact that during President Obama's second term, police shootings of Black men have emerged as a lightning rod for American race relations. After the Gates incident, the president refrained from speaking about the strained relationship between Blacks and the criminal justice system until the Trayvon Martin case. Martin's death spurred national protest and increased attentiveness to similar events occurring in municipalities across the country. Shortly after Martin's killer was found not guilty, the movie *Fruitvale Station* was released, a fictionalized dramatization of the murder of Oscar Grant by Bay Area Rapid Transit Police that was caught on tape by onlookers on the platform.[6] Though Grant was killed years before Martin, his case remained a hot-button issue in the Bay Area and was inserted into the national spotlight when the critically acclaimed movie was released shortly after the Martin verdict (Scott 2013). After these highly visible cases shone light on the issue, it seemed as if accounts about the murder of unarmed Blacks, mostly men, flooded into the American spotlight and nightly news programs. The news website *Gawker* provided a photo display of seventy-six unarmed people of color killed by police since 1999 that was compiled by the NAACP Legal Defense and Education Fund (Juwiak and Chan 2014). Fifty-one of the seventy-six (67 percent) were killed during Obama's presidency. Because national records are not kept, it is hard to know whether this represents an increase or decline. The innovation that makes collection of data about such incidents possible seemed to be the use of smart phones and social media by people who witnessed such murders. After a few cases received national attention, additional attention was paid to others.

Black America's attention to these kinds of shootings had become more focused in light of the Martin case. Organizations such as the Dream Defenders were formed to keep the spirit of Trayvon Martin and others like him alive. The young activists in the Dream Defenders occupied the Florida statehouse for thirty-one days, demanding that the governor call a special session of the legislature to repeal the state's stand-your-ground law, which authorizes individuals to defend themselves against perceived threats with lethal force and without a duty to retreat when threatened. The effort was unsuccessful, but the Dream Defenders emerged as an important youth activist organization that quickly expanded its reach around the state and the nation (McCrory 2013). Although minor protests continued after subsequent police shootings of Blacks, nationwide protests erupted after eighteen-year-old Mike Brown was shot by Ferguson police officer Darren Wilson on August 9, 2014. Many of the bystanders shot video footage of Brown's body lying in the middle of the street for hours (Eckholm 2014). Through social media, word of the shooting spread quickly and eventually the Twitter thread about the incident became newsworthy enough for the national media. Eyewitnesses reported that Mike Brown was holding his hands up and asking the Darren Wilson not to shoot him when he was fatally wounded.

"Hands Up, Don't Shoot" became a rallying cry for protests that erupted immediately in Ferguson and expanded across the nation (Moyer and Bever 2014). Although the focus of the protests was the killing of Mike Brown, several parallel conversations began to emerge surrounding the incident. First, there were questions about the demeanor of the police during the protest. Viewers watched as police used the same equipment American soldiers used in places such as Afghanistan and learned the names of high-tech military equipment that the federal government had provided to police. American citizens were tear-gassed as tanks and armored vehicles were used to disperse protesters, and reporters wore gas masks and body armor as they captured the events live (Levs 2014). For the first time, audiences became aware that surplus military equipment was being transferred to local police departments and that police personnel were being given very little training and oversight. The optics of these nights looked like the protests Americans had watched happen in less democratic nations around the world where the military and the government are one and the same. Ferguson, Missouri, however, was a midwestern American suburb.

A second question that many people in Ferguson began to ask was whether the president would or should come to Ferguson. Obama made it clear that he was monitoring events but had no plans to go there. The president had debated whether or not to go to Ferguson with top officials, including his highest-ranking African American advisors, Attorney General Holder and Valerie Jarrett. They all agreed that "it was too messy" (Epstein and Brown 2014). *Washington Post* reporter Vincent Bzdek (2014) suggested that the president's refusal to get involved in Ferguson was directly related to the fallout from his defense of Henry Louis Gates Jr. Bdzek pointed out,

In 2009, when Harvard professor Henry Louis Gates Jr. was arrested
by Cambridge police for breaking into his own house, Obama criticized the arrest and the response by police, and immediately took
flak from law enforcement organizations for bringing race into it
when they felt like they were just doing their jobs. Obama later said
he regretted his comments, and has shied away from stepping in
when similar flashpoints have flared up. His counselors have generally warned him to stay above these frays, to remain once-removed
and presidential about them.

According to this reporter and several others, the president had
learned from the Gates incident to avoid situations like Ferguson.[7]
This time he took a new tactic by sending Attorney General Eric
Holder, whom people framed as his surrogate race man. *The
National Review* called him Obama's enforcer (Fund and von
Spakovsky 2014). Attorney General Holder was seen as someone
who could deal directly with racial issues and Black people in ways
the president could not (Nakamura and Henderson 2014). At the
time, Holder was a lame duck attorney general who would soon be
leaving his post. He also had a reputation for speaking his mind,
much to the chagrin of Republicans in Congress and conservative
media commentators. In many ways, Holder was emboldened and
empowered to speak about race.

> For Holder, Ferguson has been another example of his penchant to
> go further and say more on racial issues than President Obama is
> politically willing or able to do, particularly in giving voice to the
> anger in black communities over racial bias. Over the past 12 days,
> the nation's first African American attorney general has sounded
> sharper and more personal notes of frustration and anger than the

president—a trait that has marked his 5 1/2 years in office. (Nakamura and Henderson 2014)

The trip to Ferguson was not without incident for Holder. He
encountered angry and beleaguered Black citizens, was the target of protests, dealt with officials on the ground, and walked
the streets of Ferguson (Yan and Shoichet 2014). The people of
Ferguson openly expressed disappointment that the president
had not shown up. Nearly three months after Mike Brown's death,
President Obama invited Ferguson activists and traditional civil
rights leaders to the White House to discuss the protests (Davis
2014). There were discussions about which activists were left
out, who was included, and whether or not the demands of the
young activists could be fully expressed in the formal setting of a
White House meeting (Reilly and Bendery 2014). Ferguson and
Ferguson-inspired protests continue as young activists have die-ins
and shut down highways, railway stations, and other thorough-
fares and disrupt public events. Multiple groups broadly organize
around the hashtag and slogan #BlackLivesMatter and continue to
push for police reform and other issues.

As President Obama closes out his last term, he contends with
the same racial issue he started with—the relationship between
Blacks and law enforcement. This issue presented his first opportunity to bridge the gap between the races by skillfully articulating the perspectives of each side and identifying a common
position that all parties could agree with. Because of long-standing
polarization on this issue, it is difficult to say what that position
would look like. However, if anyone was supposed to know, it was
Obama. People expected that his race-whisperer status would give
him some insight. He had been portrayed as a racially unifying
force during the 2008 election by most mainstream media out-

lets and pundits and as a racial demagogue by the extreme right. This incident was essentially a test of both theories. It would seem that the extreme right prevailed because they essentially hobbled his ability to broach this topic again with their outsized reaction, and succeeded at this because of Obama's reluctance to provoke them further on the issue. He started his presidency with an unexpected question that led to spontaneous remarks that were intensely scrutinized. Now, at the end of his presidency, this issue has become a key part of the daily news cycle and all police shootings of unarmed people of color warrant mention. Instead of speaking directly to the issue, Obama has chosen to maintain a presidential distance by monitoring events from the White House and holding formal meetings. Moreover, while he was criticized (primarily by whites and conservatives) for acting too soon and without enough information in response to Professor Gates, he was heavily criticized (primarily by Blacks and liberals) after Ferguson for not being attentive or proactive enough. These key differences represented a clear change in fortunes for the president.

Conclusion

On November 24, 2014, around 10 p.m., the split-screen coverage on MSNBC was dystopic and surreal. Our nation's first African American president was on half of the screen while Black bodies were being restrained and contained by police officers, weaponry, and barricades on the other. As audiences watched police officers fully armored in riot gear push back crowds, arrest protestors, and pepper spray and tear gas the entire community, they also watched what race relations had come to during this historic presidency. It was a sad end to his administration's actions and words about race. This incident presented completely differently than the context that generated his first comments on race as president, when he spoke in 2009 about the arrest of Harvard professor Henry Louis Gates Jr. Three years later, President Obama spoke about race again in reaction to the not-guilty verdict in the death of Trayvon Martin. In 2014, President Obama's response to the shooting of Mike Brown was on everyone's mind and received an enormous amount of attention. The killing of Mike Brown was made more complicated by the facts of the case, Brown's social location, and the rapid changes in the racial terrain that had emerged in the intervening years of the Obama presidency. All of these examples resonate with what has come to be my understanding of Obama and race.

The thread that linked all of these Black men—President Obama, Professor Gates, Trayvon Martin, and Michael Brown—was really the question of belonging. That question haunts the lives of Black men and boys and all African Americans through their personal and collective histories. Where do Black bodies belong? Who maps the cartography of Black lives? Who controls these spaces and what rights are owed and offered there? Which inhabitants are worthy of protection by and from those who govern? How are punishments for transgressions meted out? Are they fair? Is fairness a possibility? What can be done to challenge oppression and injustice? These questions are so old and so entrenched in the social schema of Black people that for the dominant group, they become tiresome and sometimes move to the periphery. But the power of these questions is the speed at which they can command center stage in American life. They have the power to deliver a sucker punch to comfort and complacency. In some ways, the historic election of 2008 provided the perception of a moment of refuge from the tumult of American racial politics. In little ways, that perception of a coming era of racial unity began eroding on election night 2008, and the split screen on the night of the grand jury decision in the death of Mike Brown threatened to undo much of the progress Obama's election had made.

Belonging in Society

The controversy surrounding Mike Brown's death is essentially about whether the actions of the police officer who shot him were justified. The Black community clearly believes that they were not. As is the case for most current events, many smart phones recorded aspects of the incident, and those recordings were shared with law enforcement, lawyers, the media, and the general public. Also as expected, the videos, the credibility of the witnesses, and the worthiness of the victim all came under scrutiny as evidence was collected, narratives were framed by the police and the victim's family, and the nation watched.

Interestingly, and sadly, the entire interaction between Michael Brown and Office Darren Wilson began because of a question of belonging. Michael Brown and his friend, Dorian Johnson, were walking down the middle of a residential street talking and joking like many teenagers in many American neighborhoods. When Officer Wilson saw them, because formal laws do not allow people to walk in the street, he ordered them onto the sidewalk. This is an example of formal versus informal codes and norms. Although walking in the middle of a residential street is illegal, doing so where there are no cars or traffic does not generally rise to the point of police action. Kids play in neighborhood streets across the nation. Neighborhood associations erect signs asking drivers to slow down and be mindful that there are children at play in their community. Making spaces open and safe for community children is a norm that often trumps legal requirements to keep the streets clear. However, for Blacks, even in their own community, their right to belong is obstructed by state surveillance. Officer Wilson yelled at the two young men to get out of the street, in essence telling them that they did not belong there. From this initial assumption about belonging, the situation escalated, and in rapid succession, there was a scuffle, a chase, and a dead child lying on the ground in full view of his entire community for hours.

Many of the activists who called for the president to be more involved in Ferguson were young people who had cut their political teeth during protests surrounding the death of Trayvon Martin. The level of attention Martin's death received can be almost completely credited to the power of social media to keep stories alive and shape current news trends. Community activist marshalled the power of social media to change the actions of the state, which was forced to investigate more, arrest Martin's killer, and bring him to trial. Like the death of Mike Brown, Martin's death was also about

Black bodies and belonging. George Zimmerman saw a child moving through his gated community and made an assumption that he did not belong because a Black teenager in a hoodie did not fit with his vision of his community. So sure was Zimmerman that Martin was out of place that he ignored the directions of the emergency dispatcher to stop following Martin and wait for trained, *actual* police officers. The sadness of this story is compounded by the fact that the police officers on the scene were as clear as Zimmerman that Treyvon Martin did not belong in that community. Though Martin died within shouting distance of his father's house, there was no door-to-door canvas to investigate whether or not the victim was on his way to one of the condominiums in the complex. Tracy Martin, Trayvon Martin's father, found his son by calling the police and filing a missing person's report the following morning. The police then informed him of the unidentified teen who had been brought in the night before and he was transported to the morgue to identify his son (Robles 2012; Botelho 2012). Law enforcement officials, crime scene investigators, and other officials on the scene all treated Trayvon Martin as if he was an interloper. The process by which Martin's death was handled the night he died was a ritual reserved for trespassing strangers who challenged the community's attempts to be a "peaceful" oasis; they were not the procedures that would have been used for a child who had been senselessly killed in his own neighborhood.

To an enormous degree, where individuals landed on the questions of Zimmerman's innocence or guilt was based on three concepts—race, attire, and belonging. If you, like Zimmerman, understood that a Black body moving through a gated condo community was out of place, then you were more likely to sympathize with him. If you, like Martin's advocates, believed that there were no boundaries to spaces that Black bodies can inhabit, you saw

Martin's death as a clear case of murder. The fact that a jury found Zimmerman not guilty did very little to change the hearts and minds of either camp.

The president expressed enormous grief over the death of Trayvon Martin. It was this death that broke Obama's public silence on race and the criminal justice system. Trayvon Martin's death seemed to break the embargo on speaking about these issues that President Obama and his advisors imposed after the Gates arrest. Clearly, the incident with Professor Gates had not cost Gates his life, and there was no indication on either side that the interaction ever came close to that point. However, there was no reason to believe that a kid going to a convenient store or another kid walking in the middle of his street would cost them their lives either. In each of these interactions, including the one with Professor Gates, the problem was never solely about the perceived infractions. Instead, the issue was about transgressions in the context of not belonging. It was about living in worlds where Black males embodied strangers and, more specifically, danger.

Professor Gates was arrested in his own home because police were told there was a raced and gendered body on the porch that did not match the address. This, President Obama understood very well. He spent his academic life in halls and porches where people questioned his right to exist there. He spoke about this at relatively great length when asked about Professor Gates's arrest. He knew the assumption that a Black male didn't belong in a middle- or upper-class setting well and took issue with the police officer for not defusing the matter the moment the assumption of intrusion had been disproven. African Americans know that there is no context in which whites feel prohibited from asking for Blacks for identifying documents. Monitors stroll into Black polling stations to oversee Blacks who are exercising their hard-fought right to vote. Whites ask Blacks to prove they belong in the political sphere with increasingly stringent voter ID laws, and the Supreme Court abets their efforts through decisions that undermine the Voting Rights Act. Cops stop African Americans for living in spaces where Black bodies are unexpected. Whites feel free to ask Blacks to demonstrate their right to exist, to control, and to lead in spaces where they do not expect to see them. It has become enduringly apparent that Black bodies are constrained within boundaries that are circumscribed by white whims and white visions of liberty.

Belonging in the White House

The questioning of Gates's right to be on his own porch and to pry his own door open is etched in many people's memory of the Obama presidency. The fact that we even know about Gates's arrest is the product of a historical novelty. A Black Ivy League professor who gets into a minor scrape with a small-town police officer would not normally be newsworthy. But this Black Ivy League professor could relate his experience to his friend, the first African American president of the United States. Barack Obama was already engaged in his own project of belonging. He had already spent the better part of two years running a near-perfect campaign to convince Americans that he belonged in the White House. Barack Obama's election required Americans to support a different vision for political leadership. In the intervening days between his election and his inauguration, there was a significant amount of self-congratulatory rhetoric about the ability of America to change and adapt to newer and greater challenges. In many ways, President Obama began a new project after the election: convincing the American people that he belonged in the highest seat of power.

This book is an exploration of how President Obama persuaded the American people to believe that he belonged in a place where the interactive effects of his raced and gendered body did not fit the space he was trying to inhabit.

President Obama was able to strategically employ diverse racial narratives to attract multiple and sometimes divergent groups. Unlike white candidates, he did not use (implicit or explicit) racist tropes to demobilize white liberals or mobilize white conservatives. For the most part, he also did not use racial narratives to inoculate himself from the racist fears of white voters, at least not in the way it was traditionally done by candidates of color. Barack Obama's use of race to achieve political victory turns our understanding of the deployment of race in campaigns on its head. The kind of race talk he employed illustrated an ability to authentically engage with multiple and sometimes competing racial histories. It represented the maturity of some old techniques African American candidates used in efforts to deracialize their campaigns, but it extended and reshape the tools beyond mere erasure of racial threat. Obama used the key deracialization method of focusing on the personal uplift story of the candidate to a greater advantage than any other candidate before him. Part of his ability to do that was attributable to his multiracial heritage. He has real connections to more than just African American history, which is mired in a struggle for recognition and calls into question key propositions of American democratic principles.

The fact that Barack Obama has a diverse racial heritage is interesting but completely out of his control. President Obama uses his understanding of how race underscores meaning and emotions in American life in myriad ways, and he uses that knowledge to achieve political ends. He is well versed in dominant racial tropes and uses them strategically to attract groups for whom each trope resonates. The president is skilled at finessing historical moments and their meaning to convince potential supporters that their "shared" social connection has a larger political meaning. He acknowledges the way he changes the rhythm, tone, and style of his speech when addressing African American audiences, and it is quite probable that he does something similar with other groups. He used these tropes as instruments to recruit supporters during elections. Each instrument (i.e., each racial trope) has its own imagery, its own themes, and a particular audience for whom it resonates, and knowing which instrument to choose for each collection of voters is as important as understanding that the instruments exist. This twofold process—understanding the impact of racial tropes and knowing how and when to use them—has never been embodied in one candidate to such a large degree. The number of instruments he can use to authentic and successful effect is unprecedented.

What is also important to note here is that even among various identity groups and the racial tropes associated with them, there are degrees of freedom related to how one can talk about them. Barack Obama did not use every single part of his personal history in campaigns; instead, he focused on the aspects of his life and career that would inform voters about his character and his leadership skills. He also made choices about how he told each story. He didn't just tell these stories; he framed each story to produce a desired effect.

Overview of Analysis

In chapter 1, I began with the racial community with which President Obama self-identifies—African American—in an effort to understand his use of Black pathology narratives. I argue that his choice to repeatedly chastise Blacks for everything from how they rear children to the political choices they make served two important purposes. First, he was not just a political unknown to whites; he was also a stranger to Blacks. This meant that he needed to establish himself within his own racial group as well. Engaging in these "tough love" conversations was the political equivalent of keeping it real. He was doing what many others in the African American community had done before him. He engaged in difficult conversations about the things Blacks could do for themselves to improve their own condition, and Blacks cheered him on as a community insider who really understood the Black community— his community. However, those difficult dialogues also form the core of many whites' beliefs about why Blacks have not progressed more. Whites tend to believe that if Blacks worked harder, they would have better outcomes, in the same ways Barack Obama prescribed. Consequently, watching Obama upbraid his community demonstrated to whites that he had some clarity about the factors contributing to persistent racial inequality. Because both Blacks and whites supported his arguments about Black pathology, there was very little push back when Obama used such narratives. The context in which he offered the racial narrative was important. He offered these comments to majority-Black audiences who were clapping in support, and he offered them as if he was saying them in a homogenous racial space. But he was not. His words were broadcasted on television so viewers across the nation could hear and make assessments about the veracity of his words. This extra layer of surveillance changed the nature of the interaction and provided fodder for negative perceptions about Blacks. However, because the visual images that accompanied his speech suggested what he was doing was appropriate and the words fit with popular beliefs, Obama received virtually no criticism for his statements.

In chapter 2, I examined how Obama connects to whiteness by focusing on patriotic iconography most closely associated with white Americans. He used narratives about his grandfather's military service and his grandmother's factory work during World War II as examples of the kinds of values that were instilled in him. He was raised by members of the greatest generation, and because they passed their core values to him, he understands the importance of sacrifice and love of country. Obama reserved these stories for occasions when he was addressing majority-white audiences or veterans or for small, intimate fund-raisers. He did not use this narrative with Blacks because he understood that the Black community's experience with military service was very complex for soldiers who fought simultaneously against racism at home and fascism abroad. President Obama also used his grandparents' story as a prototypical story of American progress and exceptionalism. The Dunhams served and sacrificed, and when the war was over they were rewarded with the GI Bill and a VA home loan. One of the reasons they could access these veterans' benefits and improve their future was because they were white. Blacks were systematically discriminated against in these very same programs. It is understandable that Obama appreciates and respects his grandparents' valor and sacrifice, but the fact that he told that narrative without complicating the story to account for the experiences of Black soldiers is telling. He intentionally tapped into a form of patriotic whiteness that allows him access to a particular historical moment that has since been commemorated with an almost religious zeal. That rhetorical choice served to mobilize white voters, but it did so at the expense of a factual understanding of the historical moment.

Chapter 3 analyzed the political impact of President Obama's "A More Perfect Union" speech. This speech was important because he made it at a critical juncture in the 2008 campaign when negative racial associations threatened to derail the work he'd done to become the Democratic Party nominee. It was also important because it provided the most detailed insight into his beliefs about how race works in America. The speech did the work it needed to do by defusing a volatile political moment, but it did so at a cost. Much of the imagery he used in the speech diminished the importance of key differences in racial perspectives by equating conflicting ideas and events and mischaracterizing historical moments to fit his rhetorical needs. His speech presents great challenges for racial reconciliation in America. The president's words were soothing to most viewers and successfully persuaded white voters not to withdraw their support, but he did so by smoothing over deep chasms in U.S. political culture and policies. For example, he suggested that the rift between those who support affirmative action policies and those who are enraged by them could somehow be bridged. And while he provided a vision of a future characterized by increased racial harmony and intergroup cooperation, the only group for which he provided specific instructions about the things they needed to change to make this vision a reality was African Americans. Even in his view of a more harmonious racial future, African Americans must overcome their tendency toward Black pathology.

In chapter 4, I examined the fallout from President Obama's first "racial incident" in the White House—his response to the arrest of Harvard Professor Henry Louis Gates Jr. When the president scolded a small-town police officer for arresting Professor Gates in his own home, he set off a firestorm of controversy about his ability to lead and his views on race. Conservatives used this moment, quite successfully, to stifle the president's ability to be an effective public advocate for any issues tied directly to the Black community. Conservative pundits and media outlets engaged in extensive discussions about whether or not the president's response indicated a deeper hostility toward white people. For them, his opposition to the actions of Officer Crowley was really opposition to blue-collar salt-of-the-earth working white Americans, and they registered this belief early and often. The president's spontaneous comment about the arrest of a friend also signaled to his detractors that he was ill equipped to lead the most powerful nation on earth. Conservatives asked whether the president could demonstrate restraint in the face of such a difficult job. They concluded that he could not. Concerns about Obama's handling of the incident were not limited to conservatives. Public opinion polls taken at the time reflected whites' strong disapproval of Obama's remarks about the Gates incident regardless of party affiliation, and for several weeks, coverage of the president's response to the Gates incident preempted coverage of his most important public policy project—health care reform. Obama learned in this moment that advocating for Blacks would be quite difficult and that doing it as president would have the effect of overshadowing all other policy discussions. The president did not address the issues of African Americans and policing again until July 2013, when George Zimmerman was found not guilty of killing Trayvon Martin.

The Race Whisperer and the Future of Black Politics

When Jesse Jackson ran for president in 1984 and 1988, an important side effect was the formation of a cohort of African Americans interested in seeking elective office. They learned about the campaign process through organizing for Jackson and other Black candidates during that period. But Jackson was also important because his successes and failures modeled the process for future

Black candidates. To what extent can Barack Obama serve as a similar model? The problem with relying on the personal narratives of candidates as models for political success is that they are difficult to replicate. Thus, individuals who seek to emulate Obama must find equally interesting sources within their own personal narratives to illustrate the characteristics that are deemed important for leadership. Obama's personal narrative is particularly unique, and it enables him to move across racial groups and tap into narratives that are normally not possible for African American candidates. This sets him apart from most potential Black candidates who seek to use his strategy as a model.

What might be more replicable, however, is his clear understanding of how to use racial tropes strategically to convey important messages. A candidate's racial history can illustrate belonging and competency in the same way that their family demonstrates stability or military service indicates patriotism. Barack Obama expanded the role of race in American campaigns in ways that force observers to rethink our analyses of race and candidates. He was more than just a typical deracialized candidate trying to steer clear of racially divisive topics. While he has not been eager to deal with racial questions directly, he engaged in a sophisticated engagement with voters using narratives that were steeped in racial significance.

Black politics scholars are constantly attentive to the practical utility of what they study for the Black community. They have a desire to understand the political world in which African Americans find themselves and how Blacks, as a collective, can best improve their standing in that world. From the time Barack Obama announced that he was running for president and as his campaign became increasingly viable, energetic discussions were held to debate what his rise to power meant for the political advancement of African Americans. The clearest conclusion that can be drawn from the case studies in this book is that in the current racial landscape, having an African American president does not bring the country closer to increased racial harmony or Black political empowerment. In fact, a Black president seemed to have a more difficult time than other presidents taking positions that might lead to Black political progress, even when the position he took was one that most Americans would support were it not for race. Advocating for Blacks has been a difficult prospect for President Obama, and this has created particular problems for him given the high level of Blacks' expectations of what he could do for them as president. No one believed that he would provide a panacea for racial problems that are centuries old, but some thought that he would at least be able to articulate the preferences of African Americans and the challenges they face to the American public.

His first effort to articulate a long-standing grievance between Blacks and the police—in the context of the arrest of Professor Gates—may have been poorly worded, but it was an attempt to make the differing perspectives clear. His political opponents immediately saw his effort as evidence of hostility toward whites, and whites across party lines felt rebuffed by his "teachable moment." I believe that he could have been a strong and outspoken advocate for Blacks from the White House; he could have made choices that were explicit nods to the Black community. He has been able to introduce policies that addressed the concerns of other constituencies. For example, the Dream Act, a reform of immigration policy that would allow undocumented citizens who were brought to the United States as children to gain legal status, was intended to solidify support among immigrant groups, especially Latinos. The president also announced that he had changed his opinion on gay marriage and took steps to make sure that the same-sex spouses of federal employees receive the same benefits as the spouses of heterosexual employees. This directly addressed a major concern of the LGBT community. Both of these policies came at great political risks. However, addressing Blacks as a core constituency to whom he is beholden because of their electoral support came at an exceptionally high cost. He learned that quickly from the Gates incident. After that, he did not introduce a major policy that would have impacted African Americans, with the exception of the My Brothers' Keeper program late in his second term, which also included Latinos.

This is not to suggest that African Americans have not benefited from election of the first Black president. Race has shaped perceptions of Obama's presidency in both symbolic and substantive ways. Seeing an African American occupy the highest office in the nation has created role models for Black children, increased Black access to the White House, and demonstrated that racial barriers are continuing to be dismantled. This book is concerned with how Obama uses race and the ways that his racial rhetoric is constrained. If, as I argue, he is really required to maintain a political distance from Black issues, then Blacks have been denied more substantial political gains during his presidency. It also means that Blacks have needed to continue to rely on traditional strategies such as public protests and lobbying by advocacy groups to make desired political gains. However, a side effect of electing the first Black president was an unwillingness on the part of African Americans to protest in ways they had before. Elsewhere, I have argued that a protest/protection conundrum exists in the Black community's relationship with Barack Obama (Price 2011). A desire to protect the historic and racial importance of Obama's presidency trumps the need for ongoing political pressure on the office of the president to have group demands met. In many ways this left the Black community hamstrung in its ability to advocate to the nation's highest office. It was difficult for African Americans and their organizations to acknowledge the constraints of the office and their unique feelings for the officeholder at the same time. The office was still the same, and the way that Blacks engaged with it needed to remain intact. But the officeholder was now someone from their own racial group, and they needed to figure out ways to be supportive while demanding that he enumerate the ways he would advocate for them, just as he did for other groups. Sadly, this did not happen.

The fact that President Obama avoided explicit conversations about race is understandable as a personal political choice. He was not going to be elected as a pro-Black candidate. His avoidance does not mean that race disappeared from his rhetoric. Instead, we see subtler insertions of racial themes and imagery into his words and actions. Most of the imagery is revealed through his personal narratives, the identities he chooses to prioritize, and the related stories he chooses to share with audiences. *The Race Whisperer* examines how Obama uses his connection to Blackness and whiteness in order to connect with audiences and mobilize support. One could analyze how he uses other identities. How he uses his international identity from his Kenyan father and the time he spent living abroad as a child could inform an analysis of the narratives he uses to engage with immigrant populations. This is particularly the case for how he frames the Dream Act and immigration reform and his early overtures to Muslim populations. My goal in this book was to demonstrate the need for a more complicated examination of race in the Obama era beyond what racial groups Obama belongs to. I wanted to highlight Obama's understanding of the fluidity of identity categories and his skillful handling of particular racial grammars. Additionally, I wanted to draw some conclusions for what this racial moment means for Black politics beyond just electing the first Black president.

Enormous expectations were placed on Barack Obama leading up to the 2008 election, some of which he hinted at or at least let his supporters believe that he could fulfill. In particular, people expected Barack Obama to know the way forward in race relations in the United States because he was so proficient at satisfying large proportions of all races during his campaign. He was perceived as the great race whisperer. It has become clear that race whispering, at least in the way Barack Obama does it, has its costs. If Obama is the model for Black politicians going forward, then how will Black elected officials be political advocates for Black issues *and* win election to higher offices? It seems that these goals are difficult to achieve simultaneously. Race whispering requires a focus on unity in ways that can uphold the current racial order and the narratives that maintain racial hierarchies. It is often said that Obama avoided talking about race during his campaigns, but he actually talked about and around race fairly often. He made statements to the Black community that were quite insidious and even damaging to Black political efforts. These references to race were received by audiences without much critique. That absence of critique suggests that deriding Black people is an acceptable form of open race talk but other kinds must be suppressed. It also means that the way Black candidates discuss the past is constrained. Discussing the challenging experiences of Black people over the course of U.S. history means complicating the nostalgic and patriotic narratives used in campaigns. It is not clear that white voters are amenable to these more nuanced and alternative readings of history.

The Obama model also presents challenges to African American voters and political observers. Obama's candidacy inspired African Americans to participate at record levels in the election process. It also inspired great pride. However, pride and participation were accompanied by a strong reluctance to press Obama to articulate a vision for what he would do to improve the lives of Black people. He offered symbolic overtures and many African Americans imparted more meaning to them. Just as African American office seekers must garner support across multiple and competing constituencies, African American voters will also be required to pin down promises from these office seekers in the same way that other communities do. To continue to equate common racial membership with common political goals is detrimental to Black political progress. The African American community has used lobbying and protest strategies to make demands of presidential candidates and administrations since the founding of the country. When the choice seemed to be between Barack Obama's successful election and pushing Black political demands, many chose to work toward Obama's election. It proved difficult to transition from working toward Obama's electoral success to working to ensure that he was attentive to Black political processes.

As America's first Black president prepares to leave the White House, we have learned many lessons about race and politics. This book discussed many of the racial constraints that decreased Obama's ability to have more explicit conversations about race, but it is also a book about choices. If Black politics remains a group-based endeavor that is led, in part, by Black elected officials, then Black elected officials have to talk about the way certain public policies continue to have a disproportionate impact on Black communities. That is an explicit racial discussion that threatens to upset dominant perceptions and norms and potentially spurns white voters. Understanding how to simultaneously support Black candidates who run for office at the state and national level and a Black political agenda that ameliorates racial inequality is the most important challenge to emerge in the Obama era. This book analyzes important snapshots during Obama's campaign and administrations that provide some clues about how this important challenge presented itself and the resulting political fallout. As other Black candidates vie for the presidency, thinking through a Black political future under more Black presidents seems critical.

NOTES

INTRODUCTION

1 In early 2014, the Obama administration announced a new initiative called My Brother's Keeper that would develop mentoring programs and other opportunities for boys and young men of color as a way of combating negative stereotypes and disastrous demographic realities associated with this population such as high rates of incarceration and unemployment ("My Brother's Keeper" 2014). Though everyone agreed that this population needed some kind of intervention and attention, some groups were disappointed that the president chose to focus exclusively on young men of color instead of all youth. Noted legal scholar Kimberle Crenshaw (2014) spearheaded an effort (#WhyWeCantWait) that pointed out how the White House had become the "most influential supporter" of the "myth" that Black girls and women are faring better than Black men thus less deserving of similar attention.

2 See, for example, King and Smith 2011. The authors point to the ways that racial cleavages that existed prior to Obama's election in 2008 remained as an enduring feature of American political life.

3 Admittedly, *Dreams from My Father* was likely published well before Obama eyed 1600 Pennsylvania Avenue; however, sales of the book skyrocketed after he began his presidential bid.

4 It was in South Carolina during the primary where Black billionaire Bob Johnson questioned Obama's Blackness. Johnson suggested that the Clintons had been much more responsive to the needs of the Black community in the past and that Clinton was more deserving of the Black vote than Obama (Seelye 2008a).

5 This was 30 percentage points more than any other racial group and more than Kerry and Gore got in the two previous elections. In 2004, Kerry got 88 percent of the African American vote, and in 2000, Gore got 90 percent (CNN 2004).

6 Tali Mendelberg (2001) notes that is not necessarily true of voters with high levels of racial resentment.

7 Paul Frymer (1999) attributes this to the fact that African Americans are in a state of party capture, meaning they cannot leave the Democratic Party

because they have no political alternative. This leaves Democrats free to use their time and resources to battle the Republican Party for white votes.

8 The Democratic Leadership Council (DLC) positioned itself as an answer to the concerns of the moderate arm of the Democratic Party. Formed in the 1980s, the DLC "pushed balanced budgets, free trade, tough-on-crime policies, and welfare reform—all of which alienated the base, but became a key part of the Clinton's 'New Democrat' agenda and his presidential legacy" (Smith 2011; see also King and Wickham-Jones 1999).

9 According to Bright (1995, 484), "the logs at the prison showed that in Ricky Rector's last days, he was howling and barking like a dog, dancing, singing, and laughing inappropriately and saying that he was going to vote for Clinton."

CHAPTER 1. BARACK OBAMA AND BLACK BLAME

1 A July 2008 article in the *New Yorker* points to more than a half a dozen incidents on the campaign trail (Amira 2008). Entitled "Why Is Jesse So Testy? Obama's Tough Love for the Black Community," this article was published after Jesse Jackson offered harsh critique of Obama on an open microphone that Jackson believed was off.

2 Contemporary examples include Newark mayor Cory Booker, Minnesota congressman Keith Ellison, and Massachusetts governor Deval Patrick.

3 A brief list of Axelrod's clients includes former mayor of Detroit Dennis Archer, former mayor of Cleveland Michael White, former mayor of Philadelphia John Street, and former mayor of Houston Lee Brown.

4 Giddings's (1984) *When and Where I Enter*, for instance, provides a detailed history of the Black women's club movement, the primary focus of which was social service and community uplift. Beyond altruism, however, she finds that these women viewed their own progress as inextricably linked to that of the larger Black community. She quotes Mary Church Terrell, who said that "self-preservation demands that [Black women] go among the lowly, illiterate and even the vicious, to which they are bound to ties of race and sex . . . to reclaim them" (quoted in Giddings 1984, 97). Using empirical evidence, social scientists have demonstrated strong support for a belief that the lives of Blacks are inextricably connected using a concept called linked fate (Gurin, Hatchett, and Jackson 1989; Tate 1993; Dawson 1994).

5 In a *New York Times* article, Gloria Steinem (2008) criticized media pundits for unnecessarily creating conflict between female and African American voters in the Democratic primary. She pointed to the fact that Hillary Clinton had a 40 percent margin over Obama in the African American community as evidence that the election was about highly qualified candidates rather than about race or gender.

6 See "President Obama Morehouse Speech Criticized as Condescending and Inappropriate," Black Voices page of *Huffington Post*, June 5, 2013, http://www.huffingtonpost.com/2013/06/05/president-obama-morehouse-speech-criticized-_n_3392200.html.

7 Code switching happens when individuals use Standard English with strangers or in public settings and rely on vernacular language patterns, foreign languages, or accents when speaking with familiars or identity-group members. Studies find that minority students who are able to code switch usually do better in integrated schools and are seen as more likeable and more competent by their non-Black peers (Shepherd 2011; Billings 2005; Koch, Gross, and Kolts 2001).

8 Cathy Cohen (1999) has demonstrated that these agendas often privileged one particular interest over others to the detriment of the Black community's most vulnerable populations.

CHAPTER 2. BARACK OBAMA, PATTON'S ARMY, AND PATRIOTIC WHITENESS

1 It was widely reported that the president checked only one box in the 2010 census—African American—though the census allows for individuals to choose more than one race box (Smith 2010).

CHAPTER 3. BARACK OBAMA'S MORE PERFECT UNION

1 The "Bradley effect" is named after Los Angeles mayor Tom Bradley, an African American who lost the 1982 California gubernatorial race despite having been ahead in all the public opinion polls leading up to the election (Payne 2011).

2 I use the term "postfeminist" to refer to a larger phenomenon that encapsulates third-wave feminism. Genz (2006, 341) sees "an overlap between third wave feminism and postfeminism" because of "an unavoidable consequence of the social and political confusion in contemporary political culture." It represents an ideological shift toward "individual and daily gender-based struggles" (338).

3 Clearly these categories are not mutually exclusive. These identity groups represent overlapping constituencies and demands. Black feminist and queer scholars have been quite attentive to the fact that these kinds of lists can reify categories in ways that marginalize their members (Hull, Scott, and Smith 1982; Cohen 1999). This list is merely to suggest the widespread identity formations around which activists arrayed themselves and mobilized others.

4 This becomes even more difficult when the discourse of the "formerly" marginalized seems to validate a post-identity moment, while mainstream

groups take on the language of the marginalized to push through exclusionary policies and sway public opinion against previously targeted groups.

5 Springer's (2002, 1062) widely cited *Signs* essay "Third Wave Black Feminism?" discusses Black feminists' connections to discussions of third-wave feminism and ultimately argues that "as we learn more about women of color's feminist activism, the wave analogy becomes untenable." The *Signs* issue also included responses to Springer's article by second-wave Black feminist Beverly Guy-Sheftall (2002).

6 There is a prodigious amount of research on this period. For instance, see Morris's (1984) *Origins of the Civil Rights Movement*; Kluger's (2004) *Simple Justice*; or Ransby's (2003) *Ella Baker and the Black Freedom Movement*.

7 For example, the Supreme Court recently gutted the Voting Right Acts (Barnes 2013).

8 Yet compare this to Judith Warner's (2013) article "The Opt-Out Generation Wants Back In," which re-interviews women who made the choice to leave high-paying professional jobs in favor of full-time homemaking. Less than a decade later, they want their old jobs back but are finding it enormously difficult to pick up where they left their careers.

9 These changes should not be overstated. The absence of overt expressions of racism does not mean the absence of racism or racist organizing. In fact, the Southern Poverty Law Center, which tracks hate groups, reports a significant rise in hate groups and membership in these groups in the wake of Obama's election (Chen 2009).

10 Examples include cases such as *Shelby v. Holder*, which did away with key provisions of the Voting Rights Act, and *Fisher v. Texas*, which offered yet another challenge to already weakened affirmative action policies.

CHAPTER 4. AN OFFICER AND TWO GENTLEMEN

1 More recent reports have suggested that he took back his statements reluctantly and at the urging of the highest-ranking African American in his cabinet, Valerie Jarrett (Felsenthal 2014).

2 "Lee Daniels' The Butler," IMDB, accessed July 25, 2015, http://www.imdb.com/title/tt1327773/.

3 Interestingly, Limbaugh continuously referred to him as "Skippy" in a discussion about how Sgt. Crowley helped Gates, who walks with a cane, down steps at the White House as the president walked ahead of them both. In Limbaugh's (2009) eyes, this indicated that Sgt. Crowley has "more compassion for a minority than Obama."

4 Beck eventually said that he regretted these comments, but the damage had already been done (HuffPost Media 2010).

5 This was a running argument for Sarah Palin during the 2008 campaign (Hamby 2008).
6 "Fruitvale Station (2013)," directed by Ryan Coogler, IMDB, accessed July 28, 2015, http://www.imdb.com/title/tt2334649/.
7 This connection was also made by Nia-Malika Henderson (2014) at the *Washington Post*, Chuck Raasch (2014) of the *St. Louis Post-Dispatch*, Jamelle Bouie (2014) of *Slate*, and several other news outlets.

REFERENCES

Amira, Dan. 2008. "Why Jesse's Testy: Obama's 'Tough Love' for the Black Community." *New York Magazine,* July 10. Accessed on January 21, 2015. http://nymag.com/daily/intelligencer/2008/07/why_jesses_testy_obamas_tough.html.

Anderson, Benedict. 2006. *Imagined Communities: Reflections on the Origin and Spread of Nationalism.* Rev. ed. New York: Verso.

Applebome, Peter. 1992. "The 1992 Campaign: Death Penalty; Arkansas Execution Raises Questions on Governor's Politics." *New York Times,* January 25. Accessed on April 24, 2014. http://www.nytimes.com/1992/01/25/us/1992-campaign-death-penalty-arkansas-execution-raises-questions-governor-s.html.

Arnold, Chris. 2009. "Charges Against Henry Louis Gates Dropped." *NPR,* July 21. Accessed on January 1, 2016. http://www.wbur.org/npr/106860000.

Axelrod, Alan. 2006. *Patton: A Biography.* New York: Palgrave McMillan.

Bai, Matt. 2008. "Is Obama the End of Black Politics?" *New York Times Magazine,* August 6.

Bailey, Beth, and David Farber. 1993. "The 'Double-V Campaign' in WWII Hawaii: African Americans, Racial Ideology, and Federal Power." *Journal of Social History* 26 (4): 818–843.

Baim, Tracy. 2010. *Obama and the Gays: A Political Marriage.* Chicago: Prairie Avenue Productions.

Balz, Dan, and Scott Clement. 2014. "On Racial Issues, America Is Divided Both Black and White and Red and Blue." *Washington Post,* December 27. Accessed January 12, 2015. http://www.washingtonpost.com/politics/on-racial-issues-america-is-divided-both-black-and-white-and-red-and-blue/2014/12/26/3d2964c8-8d12-11e4-a085-34e9b9f09a58_story.html.

Balz, Dan, and Haynes Johnson. 2009. "How Obama Snared the Lion of the Senate." *Washington Post,* August 3. Accessed April 24, 2014. http://www.washingtonpost.com/wp-dyn/content/article/2009/08/03/AR2009080303184.html.

Banjo, Omotayo. 2013. "For Us Only? Examining the Effect of Viewing Context on Black Audiences' Perceived Influence of Black Entertainment." *Race and Social Problems* 5: 309–322.

Barnes, Robert. 2013. "Supreme Court Stops Key Part of Voting Rights Act." *Washington Post,* June 25. Accessed July 25, 2015. http://www.washingtonpost.com/politics/supreme-court-stops-use-of-key-part-of-voting-rights-act/2013/06/25/26888528-dda5-11e2-b197-f248b21f94c4_story.html.

Bennett, Michael J. 1996. *When Dreams Came True: The GI Bill and the Making of Modern America*. Washington, DC: Brassey's.

Benac, Nancy. 2009. "Obama's Grandfather's War Service Revealed." *SFGate.com*. June 7. Accessed January 22, 2015. http://www.sfgate.com/news/article/Obama-s-grandfather-s-war-service-revealed-3228354.php.

Berg, Manfred. 2011. *Popular Justice: A History of Lynching in America*. New York: Rowman and Littlefield Publishers.

BET Staff. 2008. "Obama Delivers Some Tough Love in Texas." *BET.com*, March 3. Accessed August 2, 2015. http://www.bet.com/news/news/2008/03/03/newsarticlepoliticsbarackobamatexasspeech.html.

Billings, Andrew C. 2005. "Beyond the Ebonics Debate: Attitudes about Black and Standard English." *Journal of Black Studies* 36 (1): 68–81.

Bobo, Lawrence. 1998. "Race Interests and Beliefs about Affirmative Action: Unanswered Questions and New Directions." *American Behavioral Scientist* 41: 985–1003.

Bonilla-Silva, Eduardo. 2006. *Racism without Racists: Color-Blind Racism and the Persistence of Racial Inequality in America*. Lanham, MD: Rowan and Littlefield Publishers.

Botelho, Greg. 2012. "What Happened the Night Trayvon Martin Died." *CNN*, May 23. Accessed August 2, 2015. http://www.cnn.com/2012/05/18/justice/florida-teen-shooting-details/.

Bouie, Jamelle. 2014. "Why Did Obama Say So Little about Michael Brown's Killing in Ferguson?" *Slate.com*, August 26. Accessed January 13, 2015. http://www.slate.com/articles/news_and_politics/politics/2014/08/why_barack_obama_said_so_little_about_michael_brown_s_killing_in_ferguson.html.

Brienes, Winifred. 2006. *The Trouble Between Us: An Uneasy History of White and Black Women in the Feminist Movement*. New York: Oxford University Press.

Bright, Stephen B. 1995. "The Politics of Crime and the Death Penalty: Not 'Soft on Crime,' but Hard on the Bill of Rights." *Saint Louis University Law Journal* 39: 479–503.

Brokaw, Tom. 2004. *The Greatest Generation*. New York: Random House.

Bzdek, Vincent. 2014. "Why Obama Should Go to Ferguson." *Washington Post*, November 21. Accessed January 13, 2015. http://www.washingtonpost.com/blogs/the-fix/wp/2014/11/21/why-barack-obama-should-go-to-ferguson/.

Calhoun-Brown, Allison. 1996. "African American Churches and Political Mobilization: The Psychological Impact of Organizational Resources." *Journal of Politics* 58: 935–953.

Callahan, David. 2013. "How the GI Bill Left Out African Americans." Demos Policyshop, November 11. http://www.demos.org/blog/11/11/13/how-gi-bill-left-out-african-americans.

Carmines, Edward G., and James A. Stimson. 1989. *Issue Evolution: Race and the Transformation of American.* Princeton, NJ: Princeton University Press.

Carney, Timothy P. 2012. "Carney: Obama Wants Nanny State to Guide Free Enterprise." *Washington Examiner*, July 25. Accessed August 2, 2015. http://www.washingtonexaminer.com/carney-obama-wants-nanny-state-to-guide-free-enterprise/article/2503156.

Carroll, Jason. 2008. "Behind the Scenes: Is Obama Black or Biracial?" *CNN*, June 9. Accessed July 30, 2015. http://www.cnn.com/2008/POLITICS/06/09/btsc.obama.race/index.html?iref=newssearch.

Chen, Stephanie. 2009. "Growing Hate Groups Blame Obama, Economy." *CNN*, February 26. Accessed April 19, 2012. http://articles.cnn.com/2009-02-26/us/hate.groups.report_1_hate-southern-poverty-law-center-groups?_s=PM:US.

Chester, Robert K. 2013. "'Negroes' Number One Hero: Doris Miller, Pearl Harbor, and Retroactive Multiculturalism in World War II." *American Quarterly* 65 (March): 31–61.

CNN. 2004. "Election Results: America Votes 2004." *CNN*. Accessed August 2, 2015. http://www.cnn.com/ELECTION/2004/pages/results/states/US/P/00/epolls.0.htm.

Coates, Ta-Nehisi. 2013. "How the Obama Administration Talks to Black America." *The Atlantic*, May 20. Accessed January 20, 2015. http://www.theatlantic.com/politics/archive/2013/05/how-the-obama-administration-talks-to-black-america/276015/.

———. 2014. "The Case for Reparations." *The Atlantic*, June. Accessed July 31, 2015. http://www.theatlantic.com/features/archive/2014/05/the-case-for-reparations/361631/.

Cobb, William Jelani. 2010. *The Substance of Hope: Barack Obama and the Paradox of Progress.* New York: Walker and Company.

Cohen, Cathy. 1999. *Boundaries of Blackness: AIDS and the Breakdown of Black Politics.* Chicago: University of Chicago Press.

Cooper, Brittney C. 2012. "(Un)Clutching My Mother's Pearls, or Ratchetness and the Residue of Respectability." Crunk Feminist Collective, December 31. Accessed March 28, 2014. http://crunkfeministcollective.wordpress.com/2012/12/31/unclutching-my-mothers-pearls-or-ratchetness-and-the-residue-of-respectability/.

Cooper, Frank Rudy. 2008. "Our First Unisex President? Black Masculinity and Obama's Feminine Side." *Denver University Law Review* 86: 633–661.

Cooper, Helene, and Abby Goodnough. 2009. "Over Beers, No Apologies, but Plans to Have Lunch." *New York Times*, July 30.

Cosby, Bill. 2004. "Address at the NAACP on the Fiftieth Anniversary of Brown v. Board of Education." May 17. Accessed July 25, 2015. http://www.eightcitiesmap.com/transcript_bc.htm.

Cosby, Bill, and Alvin F. Poussaint. 2007. *Come On, People: On the Path from Victims to Victors*. Nashville, TN: Thomas Nelson.

Crenshaw, Kimberle. 1991. "Mapping the Margins: Intersectionality, Identity Politics, and Violence against Women of Color." *Stanford Law Review* 43 (6): 1241–1299.

———. 2014. "The Girls Obama Forgot: My Brother's Keeper Ignores Young Black Women." *New York Times*, July 29. Accessed January 1, 2015. http://www.nytimes.com/2014/07/30/opinion/Kimberl-Williams-Crenshaw-My-Brothers-Keeper-Ignores-Young-Black-Women.html?_r=0.

Cullen, Lisa Takeuchi. 2008. "Does Obama Have an Asian Problem?" *Time Magazine*, February 18. http://content.time.com/time/politics/article/0,8599,1714292,00.html.

Davis, Julie Hirschfeld. 2014. "Obama Plans Meetings on Ferguson Unrest at the White House." *New York Times*, November 30. Accessed January 13, 2015. http://www.nytimes.com/2014/12/01/us/politics/obama-plans-meetings-on-ferguson-unrest-at-the-white-house.html.

Davis, Susan. 2009. "WSJ/NBC News Poll: Who's at Fault in Gates Arrest?" *Wall Street Journal*, July 29. Accessed August 10, 2015. http://blogs.wsj.com/washwire/2009/07/29/wsjnbc-poll-whos-at-fault-in-gates-arrest/.

Dawson, Michael C. 1994. *Behind the Mule: Class in African American Politics*. Princeton, NJ: Princeton University Press.

———. 2001. *Black Visions: The Roots of Contemporary African-American Political Ideologies*. Chicago: University of Chicago Press.

Douglass, Frederick. (1863) 2000. "Men of Color, To Arms! A Call." In *Frederick Douglass: Selected Speeches and Writings*, edited by Philip S. Foner and Yuval Taylor. Chicago: Chicago Review Press. Kindle edition.

Dowd, Maureen. 1988. "Bush Says Dukakis's Desperation Prompted Accusations of Racism." *New York Times*, October 26.

Du Bois, W. E. B. (1918) 2000a. "Close Ranks." In *Let Nobody Turn Us Around: Voices of Resistance, Reform, and Renewal, An African American Anthology*, edited by Manning Marable and Leith Mullings, 242–245. Lanham, MD: Rowman and Littlefield Publishers.

———. (1903) 2000b. "Excerpt from *The Souls of Black Folks*." In *Let Nobody Turn Us Around: Voices of Resistance, Reform, and Renewal, An African American*

Anthology, edited by Manning Marable and Leith Mullings, 221–226. Lanham, MD: Rowman and Littlefield Publishers.

Durham, Aisha, Brittney C. Cooper, and Susana M. Morris. 2013. "The Stage Hip-Hop Feminist Built: A New Directions Essay." *Signs* 38 (3): 721–737.

Eckholm, Erik. 2014. "Witness Told Grand Jury That Michael Brown Charged at Darren Wilson, Prosecutors Say." *New York Times*, November 24. Accessed January 13, 2015. http://www.nytimes.com/2014/11/25/us/witnesses-told-grand-jury-that-michael-brown-charged-at-darren-wilson-prosecutor-says.html.

Edwards, Erica. 2012. *Charisma and the Fictions of Black Leadership*. Minneapolis: University of Minnesota Press.

Eilperin, Juliet. 2013. "Morehouse Faces Controversy over Obama Critic's Role in Graduation Ceremonies." *Washington Post*, May 2. Accessed January 20, 2015. http://www.washingtonpost.com/blogs/post-politics/wp/2013/05/02/morehouse-faces-controversy-over-obama-critics-role-in-graduation-ceremonies/.

Epstein, Jennifer, and Carrie Budoff Brown. 2014. "White House Debated Ferguson Trip: White House Decided Presidential Visit Would Be Too Disruptive." *Politico.com*, December 1. Accessed January 13, 2014. http://www.politico.com/story/2014/12/obama-ferguson-community-policing-113230.html.

Equal Justice Initiative. 2015. *Lynching in America: Confronting the Legacy of Racial Terror*. Montgomery, AL: Equal Justice Initiative. Accessed July 31, 2015. http://www.eji.org/files/EJI%20Lynching%20in%20America%20SUMMARY.pdf.

Fauntroy, Michael K. 2006. *Republicans and the Black Vote*. Boulder, CO: Lynne Rienner Publishers.

Felsenthal, Carol. 2014. "Fire Valerie Jarrett: If Obama Really Wants to Shake Things Up, His Closest Advisor Should Be the First to Go." *Politico Magazine*, November 7. Accessed December 23, 2014. http://www.politico.com/magazine/story/2014/11/fire-valerie-jarrett-112659.html#.VcAT-JOmWf4.

Foner, Phillip S. 1992. *Frederick Douglass on Women's Rights*. New York: Da Capo Press.

Frank, Thomas. 2009. "The Gates of Political Distraction." *Wall Street Journal*, July 29. Accessed August 2, 2015. http://www.wsj.com/articles/SB10001424052970203609204574316441057304748.

Franklin, John Hope, and Alfred A. Moss Jr. 2000. *From Slavery to Freedom: A History of African Americans*. 8th ed. New York: Alfred A. Knopf.

Frymer, Paul. 1999. *Uneasy Alliances: Race and Party Competition in American*. Princeton, NJ: Princeton University Press.

Fund, John, and Hans A. von Spakovsky. 2014. "Obama's Enforcer." *National Review*, June 11. Accessed January 13, 2015. http://www.nationalreview.com/article/380011/obamas-enforcer-john-fund-hans-von-spakovsky.

Gaines, Kevin K. 1996. *Uplifting the Race: Black Leadership, Politics, and the Culture of the Twentieth Century.* Chapel Hill: University of North Carolina Press.

———. 2007. "The Civil Rights Movement in World Perspective." *OAH Magazine of History* 21 (1): 57–64.

Genz, Stephanie. 2006. "Third Way/ve: The Politics of Postfeminism." *Feminist Theory* 7 (3): 333–353.

Giddings, Paula. 1984. *When and Where I Enter: The Impact of Black Women on Race and Sex in America.* New York: Bantam Books.

———. 2009. *Ida: A Sword among Lions.* New York: HarperCollins.

Gilens, Martin. 1999. *Why Americans Hate Welfare: Race, Media, and the Politics of Anti-Poverty Policy.* Chicago: University of Chicago Press.

Gillespie, Andra. 2012. *The New Black Politician: Cory Booker, Newark, and Post-Racial America.* New York: New York University Press.

Goldberg, Jonah. 2008. "Obama and Transcending Race." *National Review*, November 5. Accessed July 31, 2015. http://www.nationalreview.com/corner/173462/obama-transcending-race-jonah-goldberg.

Greenlee, Sam. 1973. *The Spook Who Sat by the Door.* DVD. Directed by Ivan Dixon. Los Angeles: Monarch Home Videos.

Greenstein, Fred I. 2009. *The Presidential Difference: Leadership Style from FDR to Barack Obama.* 3rd ed. Princeton, NJ: Princeton University Press.

Gurin, Patricia, Shirley Hatchett, and James S. Jackson. 1989. *Hope and Independence: Blacks' Response to Electoral and Party Politics.* New York: Russell Sage Foundation.

Guskin, Emily, Manvish Shahid Khan, and Amy Mitchell. 2010. "The Arrest of Henry Louis Gates, Jr." Media, Race, and Obama's First Year: Pew Research Journalism Project, July 26. Accessed January 12, 2015. http://www.journalism.org/2010/07/26/arrest-henry-louis-gates-jr/.

Guy-Sheftall, Beverly. 2002. "Response from a 'Second Waver' to Kimberly Springer's 'Third Wave Black Feminism'?" *Signs* 27 (4): 1091–1094.

Halloran, Liz. 2009. "Obama Beer Summit Choices Make For a Happy Hour." *NPR*, July 30. http://www.npr.org/templates/story/story.php?storyId=111373030.

Hamby, Peter. 2008. "Palin Warns Obama Create Nanny State if Elected." *CNN Political Ticker*, October 25. Accessed August 2, 2015. http://politicalticker.blogs.cnn.com/2008/10/25/palin-warns-obama-would-create-nanny-state-if-elected/.

Hancock, Ange-Marie. 2004. *The Politics of Disgust: The Public Identity of the Welfare Queen.* New York: New York University Press.

Haney López, Ian F. 2014. *Dog Whistle Politics: How Coded Appeals Have Reinvented Racism and Wrecked the Middle Class.* New York: Oxford University Press.

Harris, Fredrick C. 1999. *Something Within: Religion in African American Political Activism.* New York: Oxford University Press.

———. 2012. *The Price of the Ticket: Barack Obama and the Rise and Decline of Black Politics.* New York: Oxford University Press.

Harris-Lacewell, Melissa V. 2006. *Barbershops, Bibles, and BET: Everyday Talk and Black Political Thought.* Princeton, NJ: Princeton University Press.

Harris-Perry, Melissa V. 2011. *Sister Citizen: Shame, Stereotypes, and Black Women in America.* New Haven, CT: Yale University Press.

Harwood, Matthew. 2008. "Obama and Mixed Race in America." *The Guardian,* April 1. Accessed December 30, 2015. http://www.theguardian.com/world/deadlineusa/2008/apr/01/obamaandmixedraceinameric.

Hayes, Christopher. 2007. "Obama's Media Maven." *Nation,* February 6. Accessed October 17, 2010. http://www.thenation.com/print/article/obamas-media-maven.

Haywood, Leslie, and Jennifer Drake. 2006. "Introduction." In *Third Wave Agenda: Being Feminist, Doing Feminism,* 4th ed., edited by Leslie Haywood and Jennifer Drake, 1–24. Minneapolis: University of Minnesota Press.

Helman, Scott. 2007. "Obama Shows an Ability to Transcend Race: Connects in Iowa on Shared Values." *Boston Globe,* August 19. Accessed July 15. http://www.boston.com/news/nation/articles/2007/08/19/obama_shows_an_ability_to_transcend_race/?page=full.

Henderson, Nia-Malika. 2014. "Obama Is Playing Small Ball on Ferguson. That's Smart." *Washington Post,* December 2. Accessed January 13, 2015. http://www.washingtonpost.com/blogs/the-fix/wp/2014/12/02/obama-is-playing-small-ball-on-ferguson-thats-smart/.

Henry, Astrid. 2004. *Not My Mother's Sister: Generational Conflict and Third Wave Feminism.* Bloomington: Indiana University Press.

Henry, Charles P., Robert L. Allen, and Robert Chrisman, eds. 2011. *The Obama Phenomenon: Toward a Multicultural Democracy.* Urbana: University of Illinois Press.

Herbert, Bob. 2005. "Impossible, Ridiculous, Repugnant." *New York Times,* October 6. Accessed April 24, 2014. http://query.nytimes.com/gst/fullpage.html?res=9C04E6DF1E30F935A35753C1A9639C8B63.

Hewitt, Nancy. 2010a. "From Seneca Falls to Suffrage? Reimagining a 'Master' Narrative in U.S. Women's History." In *No Permanent Waves: Recasting US Histories of Feminism* edited by Nancy Hewitt, 15–38. New Brunswick, NJ: Rutgers University Press.

Hewitt Nancy. 2010b. "Introduction." In *No Permanent Waves: Recasting U.S. Histories of Feminism,* edited by Nancy Hewitt, 1–14. New Brunswick, NJ: Rutgers University Press.

Higginbotham, Evelyn Brooks. 1993. *Righteous Discontent: The Women's Movement in the Black Baptist Church, 1880–1920.* Cambridge, MA: Harvard University Press.

Hohn, Maria. 2008. "'We Will Never Go Back to the Old Way Again': Germany in the African American Civil Rights Debate." *Central European History* 41 (4): 605–637.

Holmes, Steven. 2008. "Blacks Forming a Rock-Solid Bloc behind Obama." *Washington Post*, October 1. Accessed January 15, 2015. http://www.washingtonpost.com/wp-dyn/content/article/2008/09/30/AR2008093002702.html?hpid=sec-politics&sid=ST2008093002732&s_pos.

Hornick, Ed. 2008. "Poll: 'Sharp Reversal' for Obama with Latino Voters." *CNN*, July 24. http://www.cnn.com/2008/POLITICS/07/24/pew.latino.poll/index.html?iref=mpstoryview.

Houston, Charles Hamilton. (1944) 2000. "The Negro Soldier." In *Let Nobody Turn Us Around: Voices of Resistance, Reform and Renewal*, edited by Manning Marable and Leith Mullings, 339–340. Lanham, MD: Rowman and Littlefield Publishers.

Huff, Richard. 2009. "Pundit Glenn Beck Calls President Barack Obama a 'Racist,' Fox News Channel Execs Downplay Comments." *New York Daily News*, July 29. Accessed August 2. http://www.nydailynews.com/entertainment/tv-movies/pundit-glenn-beck-calls-president-barack-obama-racist-fox-news-channel-execs-downplay-comments-article-1.399396.

HuffPost Media. 2010. "Glenn Beck Regrets Calling Obama Racist: 'I Have a Big, Fat Mouth.'" *Huffington Post*, August 30. Accessed July 25, 2015. http://www.huffingtonpost.com/2010/08/29/glenn-beck-regrets-callin_n_698580.html.

Hull, Gloria T., Patricia Bell Scott, and Barbara Smith. 1982. *All the Women Are White, All the Men Are Black, but Some of Us Are Brave: Black Women's Studies*. New York: Feminist Press.

Humes, Edward. 2014. *Over Here: How the GI Bill Transformed the American Dream*. New York: Diversion Books.

Huntington, Samuel. 2005. *Who Are We? The Challenges to American National Identity*. New York: Simon and Schuster.

Inskeep, Steve. 2007. "Obama to Attend Selma March Anniversary." *NPR*, February 28. Accessed January 20, 2015. http://www.npr.org/templates/story/story.php?storyId=7630250.

Johns, Joe, and Don Lemon. 2009. "Obama: I Didn't Mean to Slight Cambridge Police." *CNN*, July 24. Accessed August 12, 2015. http://www.cnn.com/2009/US/07/24/officer.gates.arrest/

Johnson, Cedric. 2007. *From Revolutionaries to Race Leaders: Black Power and the Making of African American Politics*. Minneapolis: University of Minnesota Press.

Joseph, Peniel E. 2010. *Dark Days, Bright Nights: From Black Power to Barack Obama*. New York: Basic Civitas Books.

Juwiak, Rich, and Aleksander Chan. 2014. "Unarmed People of Color Killed by Police, 1999–2014." *Gawker.com*, December 8. Accessed January 13, 2015. http://gawker.com/unarmed-people-of-color-killed-by-police-1999–2014–1666672349.

Kates, Brian. 2009. "911 Call that Led to Arrest of Harvard University Professor Henry Louis Gates Jr. Never Mentioned Race." *New York Daily News*, July 27. Accessed July 31, 2015. http://www.nydailynews.com/news/world/911-call-led-arrest-harvard-university-prof-henry-louis-gates-jr-mentioned-race-article-1.394427.

Katznelson, Ira. 2006. *When Affirmative Action Was White: An Untold History of Racial Inequality in Twentieth-Century America*. New York: W. W. Norton.

Keeter, Scott, Juliana Horowitz, and Alec Tyson. 2008. "Young Voters in the 2008 Election." Pew Research Center for the People and the Press. Accessed October 27, 2010. http://pewresearch.org/pubs/1031/young-voters-in-the-2008-election.

Kinder, Donald R., and Allison Dale-Riddle. 2012. *The End of Race? Obama, 2008, and Racial Politics in America*. New Haven, CT: Yale University Press.

Kinder, Donald R., and Lynn Sanders. 1996. *Divided by Color: Racial Politics and Democratic Ideals*. Chicago: University of Chicago Press.

King, Desmond S., and Rogers M. Smith. 2011. *Still A House Divided: Race and Politics in the Age of Obama*. Princeton, NJ: Princeton University Press.

King, Desmond S., and Mark Wickham-Jones. 1999. "From Clinton to Blair: The Democratic (Party) Origins of Welfare to Work." *Political Quarterly* 70 (72): 62–74.

Kluger, Richard. 2004. *Simple Justice: The History of* Brown v. Board of Education *and Black America's Struggle for Equality*. New York: Vintage Press.

Koch, Lisa M., Alan M. Gross, and Russell Kolts. 2001. "Attitudes towards Black English and Code Switching." *Journal of Black Psychology* 27 (1): 29–42.

Kristol, William. 2008. "George, Abe, Rick, & Barack." *New York Times*, December 28. Accessed August 2, 2008. http://www.nytimes.com/2008/12/29/opinion/29kristol.html.

Kushner, David. 2010. *Levittown: Two Families, One Tycoon, and the Fight for Civil Rights in America's Legendary Suburb*. New York: Walker and Company.

Landler, Mark, and Michael Shear. 2013. "President Offers Personal Take on Race in U.S." *New York Times*, July 19. Accessed July 29, 2013. http://www.nytimes.com/2013/07/20/us/in-wake-of-zimmerman-verdict-obama-makes-extensive-statement-on-race-in-america.html.

Levine, Lawrence W. 2007. *Black Culture and Black Consciousness: Afro-American Folk Thought from Slavery to Freedom*. New York: Oxford University Press.

Levs, Josh. 2014. "Some 'Agitators' Arrested in Ferguson Come from across U.S." *CNN*, August 19. Accessed January 24, 2015. http://www.cnn.com/2014/08/19/us/missouri-ferguson-agitators/index.html.

Lewis-Beck, Michael, Charles Tien, and Richard Nadeau. 2010. "Obama's Missed Landslide: A Racial Cost?" *PS: Political Science and Politics* 43 (1): 69–76.

Limbaugh, Rush. 2009. "A Revealing Beer Summit Photo." RushLimbaugh. com, July 31. Accessed August 12, 2015. http://www.rushlimbaugh.com/ daily/2009/07/31/a_revealing_beer_summit_photo.

Lindsay, Jay. 2009. "Lucia Whalen, 911 Caller in Gates Case, Speaks Publicly." *Huffington Post*, August 29. Accessed July 31, 2015. http://www.huffingtonpost. com/2009/07/29/lucia-whalen-911-caller-i_n_246919.html.

Lipsitz, George. 2006. *The Possessive Investment in Whiteness: How White People Profit from Identity Politics*. Rev. ed. Philadelphia: Temple University Press.

Liu, Baodong. 2010. *The Election of Barack Obama: How He Won*. New York: Palgrave McMillan.

Logan, Enid. 2011. *"At This Defining Moment": Barack Obama's Presidential Candidacy and the New Politics of Race*. New York: New York University Press.

Lopez, Mark Hugo, and Paul Taylor. 2009. "Dissecting the 2008 Election: Most Diverse in U.S. History." Pew Research Center Report, February 29. Accessed August 2, 2015. http://pewresearch.org/files/old-assets/pdf/dissecting-2008-electorate.pdf.

MacDonald, Heather. 2009. "Promoting Racial Paranoia." *National Review*, July 24. Accessed July 31, 2015. http://www.nationalreview.com/article/227946/ promoting-racial-paranoia-heather-mac-donald.

Mane, Rebecca L. Clark. 2012. "Transmuting Grammars of Whiteness in Third-Wave Feminism: Interrogating Postrace Histories, Postmodern Abstraction, and the Proliferation of Difference in Third-Wave Texts." *Signs* 38 (1): 71–98.

Mansbridge, Peter. 2009. "Obama Beer Summit Hailed as 'Friendly.'" CBC News (World, July 30. Accessed August 2, 2015. http://www.cbc.ca/news/world/ obama-beer-summit-hailed-as-friendly-1.835290.

Marshall, Stephen. 2011. *The City on the Hill from Below: The Crisis of Prophetic Black Politics*. Philadelphia: Temple University Press.

Mayhew, David. 2004. *Congress: The Electoral Connection*. 2nd ed. New Haven, CT: Yale University Press.

McAdam, Doug. 1988. *Freedom Summer*. New York: Oxford University Press.

———. 1999. *Political Process and the Development of Black Insurgency, 1920–1970*. 2nd ed. Chicago: University of Chicago Press.

McCormick, Joseph P., and Charles E. Jones. 1993. "The Conceptualization of Deracialization." In *Dilemmas of Black Politics: Issues of Leadership and Strategy*, edited by Georgia Persons, 66–84. New York: HarperCollins.

McCrory, Kathleen. 2013. "After 31 Days, Dream Defenders End Protest at Florida Capital." *Tampa Bay Times*, August 15. Accessed Janu-

ary 13, 2015. http://www.tampabay.com/news/politics/stateroundup/
dream-defenders-ending-capitol-protest/2136646.

McDaniel, Eric L. 2008. *Politics in the Pews: The Political Mobilization of Black Churches*. Ann Arbor: University of Michigan Press.

McGowan, Sharon Sulker. 2009. "Sweet Success: Chicago Sun-Times Washington Bureau Chief Lynn Sweet Covers National Politics with a No-Holds-Barred Approach." *Northwestern Magazine* (Winter). Accessed August 2, 2015. http://www.northwestern.edu/magazine/winter2009/feature/lynnsweet.html

McIlwain, Charlton, and Stephen M. Caliendo. 2011. *Race Appeal: How Candidates Invoke Race in U. S. Political Campaigns*. Philadelphia, PA: Temple University Press.

McIntosh, Peggy. 1989. "White Privilege: Unpacking the Invisible Knapsack." *Peace and Freedom* 49 (4): 10–12.

McMillen, Sally. 2009. *Seneca Falls and the Origins of the Women's Rights Movements*. New York: Oxford University Press.

Mendelberg, Tali. 2001. *The Race Card: Campaign Strategies, Implicit Messages, and the Norm of Equality*. Princeton, NJ: Princeton University Press.

Meyer, Dick. 2004. "Bill Cosby and the Flap That Wasn't." *CNN*, May 26. Accessed November 1, 2010. http://www.cbsnews.com/stories/2004/05/26/opinion/meyer/main619640.shtml.

Mills, David. 1992. "Sista Souljah's Call to Arms." *Washington Post*, May 13.

Mitchell, Koritha. 2011. *Living with Lynching: African American Lynching Plays, Performance, and Citizenship, 1890–1930*. Urbana: University of Illinois Press.

Morris, Aldon. 1984. *The Origins of the Civil Rights Movement*. New York: Free Press.

Moyer, Justin, and Lindsey Bever. 2014. "Did Michael Brown Have His Hands Up When He Was Shot?" *Washington Post*, October 22. Accessed by January 13, 2015. http://www.washingtonpost.com/news/morning-mix/wp/2014/10/22/report-autopsy-analysis-shows-michael-brown-may-have-gone-for-darren-wilsons-gun/.

Murray, Mark. 2009. "NBC/WSJ Poll: Gates More at Fault." NBC News, July 29. Accessed August 10, 2015. http://firstread.nbcnews.com/_news/2009/07/29/4427996-nbcwsj-poll-gates-more-at-fault.

"My Brother's Keeper." 2014. White House. Accessed January 1, 2015. http://www.whitehouse.gov/my-brothers-keeper.

Nagourney, Adam. 2006. "The Pattern May Change, If . . ." *New York Times*, December 10. http://www.nytimes.com/2006/12/10/weekinreview/10nagourney.html.

Nakamura, David, and Nia-Malika Henderson. 2014. "Eric H. Holder Jr., in Ferguson, Shares Painful Memories of Racism." *Washington Post*, August 20. Accessed

January 13, 2015. http://www.washingtonpost.com/politics/eric-h-holder-jr-in-ferguson-shares-painful-memories-of-racism/2014/08/20/b05a2f62–289b-11e4–8593-da634b334390_story.html.

NBC News. 2009. "Top Cop: Officers 'Pained' by Obama Remarks." July 23. Accessed July 31, 2015. http://www.nbcnews.com/id/32092715/ns/us_news-life/t/top-cop-officers-pained-obama-remark/#.Vb-CdpOmWf4.

Nelson, William E., Jr., and Phillip Merranto. 1977. *Electing Black Mayors: Political Action in the Black Community*. Columbus: Ohio State University Press.

Newport, Michael. 2014. "Gallup Review: Black and White Attitudes towards the Police." Gallup.com. Accessed January 13, 2015. http://www.gallup.com/poll/175088/gallup-review-black-white-attitudes-toward-police.aspx.

Nielsen Company. 2011. "State of the Media: March 2011." http://www.nielsen.com/content/dam/corporate/us/en/reports-downloads/2011-Reports/State-of-the-Media-Ethnic-TV-Trends.pdf.

Niesse, Mark. 2008. "Island Life in Multiracial Hawaii Shaped Obama." *USA Today*, August 7. Accessed July 30, 2015. http://usatoday30.usatoday.com/news/politics/2008–08–07–1974308754_x.htm.

Norrell, Robert J. 2005. *The House I Live In: Race in the American Century*. New York: Oxford University Press.

Nunnally, Shayla C. 2012. *Trust in Black America: Race, Discrimination, and Politics*. New York: New York University Press.

Obama, Barack. 2004a. "Democratic National Convention Keynote Address." Boston, MA. Accessed October 18, 2010. http://www.americanrhetoric.com/speeches/convention2004/barackobama2004dnc.htm.

———. 2004b. *Dreams from My Father: A Story of Race and Inheritance*. New York: Broadway Books.

———. 2007. Barack Obama Speech—Selma, Alabama 2007. Brown Chapel, Selma, AL, March 4. http://civilrightsleader.com/barack-obama-speech-selma-alabama-2007/.

———. 2008a. *The Audacity of Hope: Thoughts on Reclaiming the American Dream*. New York: Vintage Books.

———. 2008b. "A More Perfect Union." Speech at Constitutional Hall, Philadelphia, PA, March 18. http://constitutioncenter.org/amoreperfectunion/.

———. 2008c. "Obama's Speech at the Apostolic Church of God." Father's Day, June 15. http://www.politico.com/news/stories/0608/11094.html.

———. 2009a. "Obama's Speech on 20th anniversary of the Department of Veterans Affairs as a Cabinet-Level Agency." Department of Veterans Affairs, March 16. http://www.realclearpolitics.com/articles/2009/03/obamas_remarks_on_veterans_aff.html.

———. 2009b. "President Obama's Primetime Press Conference on Health Care Reform." July 22. https://www.whitehouse.gov/video/President-Obamas-Primetime-Press-Conference-on-Health-Reform/.

———. 2009c. "Remarks by the President at the Veterans of Foreign Wars Convention." Phoenix Convention Center, Phoenix, AZ, August 17. http://www.whitehouse.gov/the-press-office/remarks-president-veterans-foreign-wars-convention.

———. 2009d. "Remarks by the President at the Congressional Black Caucus Foundation's Phoenix Awards Dinner." Washington, DC, September 27. Accessed August 2, 2015. https://www.whitehouse.gov/video/President-Obama-Speaks-at-the-Congressional-Black-Caucus-Foundation-Awards-Dinner/.

———. 2011. "Remarks by the President on the Economy in Osawatomie, Kansas." Osawatomie High School, Osawatomie, KS, December 6. http://www.whitehouse.gov/the-press-office/2011/12/06/remarks-president-economy-osawatomie-kansas.

———. 2012a. "Remarks by the President at Campaign Event in San Antonio, Texas." San Antonio, TX, July 17. http://www.whitehouse.gov/the-press-office/2012/07/17/remarks-president-campaign-event-san-antonio-tx.

———. 2012b. "Remarks by the President at Campaign Event in West Palm Beach, Florida." West Palm Beach, FL, July 19. http://www.whitehouse.gov/the-press-office/2012/07/19/remarks-president-campaign-event-west-palm-beach-fl.

———. 2013a. "Remarks by the President at Morehouse College Commencement Ceremony." Atlanta, GA, May 19. http://www.whitehouse.gov/the-press-office/2013/05/19/remarks-president-morehouse-college-commencement-ceremony.

———. 2013b. "Remarks by the President at the 'Let Freedom Ring' Ceremony Commemorating the 50th Anniversary of the March on Washington." Lincoln Memorial, Washington, DC, August 28. http://www.whitehouse.gov/the-press-office/2013/08/28/remarks-president-let-freedom-ring-ceremony-commemorating-50th-anniversa.

Obama, Michelle. 2013. "Remarks by the First Lady at Bowie State University Commencement Ceremony." Bowie, MD, May 17. http://www.whitehouse.gov/the-press-office/2013/05/17/remarks-first-lady-bowie-state-university-commencement-ceremony

O'Brien, Soledad, Gloria Borger, Candy Crowley, Jessica Yellin, Don Lemon, Tom Foreman, Dan Lothian, Wolf Blitzer, Jim Acosta, Mary Snow, Lou Dobbs, and Jeanne Moos. 2009. "White House Beer Summit." Excerpt from broadcast of *The Situation Room* (CNN), aired July 30.

Ogletree, Charles. 2012. *The Presumption of Guilt: The Arrest of Henry Louis Gates, Jr. and Race, Class, and Crime in America.* New York: Palgrave McMillan. Kindle edition.

Omi, Michael, and Howard Winant. 1994. *Racial Formation in the United States: From the 1960s to the 1990s.* New York: Routledge Press.

OpenSecrets.org. n.d. "Barack Obama (D): Candidate Summary, 2008 Cycle." Accessed October 27, 2010. http://www.opensecrets.org/pres08/summary.php?id=n00009638.

O'Reilly, Bill, Monica Crowley, and Alan Colmes. 2009. "Barack and a Hard Place: Obama Meeting with Gates, Cop; U.S. Considers Talks with Taliban." *O'Reilly Factor* (Fox News), July 29. Accessed August 2, 2015. http://www.billoreilly.com/show?action=viewTVShow&showID=2394&dest=/pg/jsp/community/tvshow-print.jsp.

Parker, Christopher. 2009. *Fighting for Democracy: Black Veterans and the Struggle against White Supremacy in the Postwar South.* Princeton, NJ: Princeton University Press.

Parks, Gregory S., and Jeffrey J. Rachlinksy. 2009. "Barack Obama's Candidacy and the Collateral Consequences of the 'Politics of Fear.'" In *Barack Obama and African American Empowerment: The Rise of Black America's New Leadership*, edited by Manning Marable and Kristen Clarke, 225–239. New York: Palgrave McMillan.

Payne, J. Gregory. 2011. "The Bradley Effect: Mediated Realities of Race and Politics in the 2008 U.S. Presidential Election." *American Behavioral Scientist* 55: 351–353.

Peoples, Whitney A. 2008. "Under Construction: Identifying Foundations of Hip-Hop Feminism and Exploring Bridges between Black Second Wave and Hip-Hop Feminism." *Meridians* 8 (1): 19–52.

Perlstein, Rick. 2012. "Exclusive: Lee Atwater's Infamous 1981 Interview on the Southern Strategy." *Nation*, November 13. Accessed April 24, 2014. http://www.thenation.com/article/170841/exclusive-lee-atwaters-infamous-1981-interview-southern-strategy.

Pew Research Center. 2008. "Obama and Wright Controversy Dominate the News Cycle." March 27. Accessed August 12, 2015. http://www.people-press.org/2008/03/27/obama-and-wright-controversy-dominate-news-cycle/.

Philpot, Tasha. 2007. *Race, Republicans, and the Return of the Party of Lincoln.* Ann Arbor: University of Michigan Press.

Politico.com. 2009. "Fox's Beck: Obama Is 'a Racist.'" Politico.com, July 28. Accessed July 25, 2015. http://www.politico.com/blogs/michaelcalderone/0709/Foxs_Beck_Obama_is_a_racist.html.

Price, Melanye T. 2009. *Dreaming Blackness: Black Nationalism and African American Public Opinion.* New York: New York University Press.

———. 2011. "Black Blame, Barack Obama, and the Future of Black Politics." In *The Black Experience in America*, edited by Edward Ramsamy and Gayle Tate, 434–448. Dubuque, IA: Kendall Hunt.

———. 2014. "Barack Obama and the Third Wave: The Syntaxes of Whiteness and Articulating Difference in the Post-Identity Era." *Politics, Groups and Identities* 2 (4): 573–588.

Raasch, Chuck. 2014. "Obama's Role in Ferguson Complicated." *St. Louis Post-Dispatch*, December 8. Accessed by January 13, 2015. http://www.stltoday. com/news/local/govt-and-politics/obama-s-role-in-ferguson-is-complicated/ article_5ca3679e-91fc-576b-b94f-c1542eff9c02.html.

Ransby, Barbara. 2003. *Ella Baker and the Black Freedom Movement: A Radical Democratic Vision*. Chapel Hill: University of North Carolina Press.

Reed, Adolph L. 1986. *The Jackson Phenomenon: The Crisis of Purpose in American Politics*. New Haven, CT: Yale University Press.

Reeves, Keith. 1997. *Voting Hopes or Fears? White Voters, Black Candidates, and Racial Politics in America*. New York: Oxford University Press.

Reilly, Ryan, and Jennifer Bendery. 2014. "Ferguson Activists, Encouraged by White House Meeting, Still Predict Uphill Battle." *Huffington Post*, December 2. Accessed January 24, 2015. http://www.huffingtonpost.com/2014/12/02/ferguson-white-house_n_6257306.html.

Remnick, David. 2008. "The Joshua Generation: Race and the Campaign of Obama." *New Yorker*, November 17. http://www.newyorker.com/ magazine/2008/11/17/the-joshua-generation.

Rivers, Caryl. 2008. "Does Obama Transcend Race?" *Huffington Post*, April 9. Accessed July 31, 2015. http://www.huffingtonpost.com/caryl-rivers/does-obama-transcend-race_b_95898.html.

Robbins, Liz. 2009. "Officer Defends Arrest of Harvard Professor." *New York Times*, July 23. Accessed July 31, 2015. http://www.nytimes.com/2009/07/24/ us/24cambridge.html?pagewanted=all&_r=0.

Roberts, John W. 1990. *From Trickster to Badman: The Black Folk Hero in Slavery and Freedom*. Philadelphia: University of Pennsylvania Press.

Robles, Frances. 2012. "A Look at What Happened the Night Trayvon Martin Died." *Tampa Bay Times*, April 2, Accessed August 2, 2015. http://www.tampabay.com/news/publicsafety/ crime/a-look-at-what-happened-the-night-trayvon-martin-died/1223083.

Roediger, David. 2005. *Working Toward Whiteness: How America's Immigrants Became White, The Strange Journey from Ellis Island to the Suburbs*. Cambridge, MA: Basic Books.

———. 2007. *The Wages of Whiteness: Race and the Making of the American Working Class*. New York: Verso.

Rothstein, Richard. 2014. "The Making of Ferguson: Public Policies at the Roots of Its Troubles." Economic Policy Institute. Accessed July 31, 2015. http://www.epi.org/publication/making-ferguson/#examining-the-distinct-public-policies-that-have-enforced-segregation.

Rustin, Bayard. 2003. "From Protest to Politics: The Future of the Civil Rights Movement." In *Time on Two Crosses: The Collected Writings of Bayard Rustin*, edited by Devon Carbado and Don Weise, 116–129. New York: Cleis Publishing.

Salsberg, Bob, and Denise Lavoie. 2009. "Mass Police Unions Ask President Obama for an Apology in Henry Louis Gates Arrest." Masslive.com, July 24. Accessed August 2, 2015. http://www.masslive.com/news/index.ssf/2009/07/mass_police_unions_ask_preside.html.

Schorr, Daniel. 2008. "A New, Post-Racial Political Era in America." NPR News Analysis, January 28. http://www.npr.org/templates/story/story.php?storyId=18489466.

Schwartz, Barry. 1996. "Memory as a Cultural System: Abraham Lincoln in World War II." *American Sociological Review* 61 (5): 908–927.

Scott, A. O. 2013. "A New Year, and a Last Day Alive: 'Fruitvale Station' Is Based on the Life of Oscar Grant III." *New York Times*, July 11. Accessed January 13, 2014. http://www.nytimes.com/2013/07/12/movies/fruitvale-station-is-based-on-the-story-of-oscar-grant-iii.html?_r=0.

Scott, James. 1992. *Domination and the Arts of Resistance: Hidden Transcripts*. New Haven, CT: Yale University Press.

Seelye, Katharine Q. 2008a. "BET Founder Slams Obama in South Carolina." *New York Times*, January 13.

———. 2008b. "In South Carolina, A Bid for Black Women's Votes." *New York Times*, January 14.

Serwer, Adam. 2008. "Obama's Racial Catch-22." *American Prospect*, August 4. prospect.org/article/obamas-racial-catch-22.

Shepherd, Michael A. 2011. "Effects of Ethnicity and Gender on Teachers' Evaluations of Students' Spoken Responses." *Urban Education* 46 (5): 1011–1028.

Simon, Scott. 2009. "Is Obama's Image Stained by Gates Controversy?" *Weekend Edition Saturday*, July 25. Accessed August 11, 2015. http://www.npr.org/templates/story/story.php?storyId=107006718.

Simpson, William M. 1994. "A Tale Untold? The Alexandria, Louisiana, Lee Street Riot (January 10, 1942)." *Louisiana History: Journal of the Louisiana Historical Association* 35 (2): 133–149.

Sinclair-Chapman, Valeria, and Melanye Price. 2008. "Black Politics, the 2008 Election, and the (Im)possibility of Race Transcendence." *PS: Political Science and Politics* 41 (4): 739–745.

Smith, Ayana. 2005. "Blues, Criticism, and the Signifying Trickster." *Popular Music* 24 (2): 175–191.

Smith, Ben. 2011. "The End of the Democratic Leadership Council Era." *Politico,* February 7. Accessed April 24, 2014. http://www.politico.com/news/stories/0211/49041.html.

Smith, Ben, and Jonathan Martin. 2008. "Why Obama Won." *Politico,* November 5. http://www.politico.com/news/stories/1108/15301.html.

Smith, Mark. 2010. "Obama Census Choice: African American." *Huffington Post,* June 2. Accessed January 9, 2015. http://www.huffingtonpost.com/2010/04/02/obama-census-choice-afric_n_524012.html.

Smith, Robert. 1996. *We Have No Leaders: African Americans in the Post–Civil Rights Era.* Albany: State University of New York Press.

Smith, Rogers. 1999. *Civic Ideal: Conflicting Visions of Citizenship in U. S. History.* New Haven, CT: Yale University Press.

Sniderman, Paul, and Thomas Piazza. 1993. *The Scar of Race.* Cambridge, MA: Harvard University Press.

Snyder, R. Claire. 2008. "What Is Third-Wave Feminism? A New Directions Essay." *Signs* 34 (1): 175–196.

Springer, Kimberly. 2002. "Third Wave Black Feminism?" *Signs* 27 (4): 1059–1082.

Squires, Catherine R. 2002. "Rethinking the Black Public Sphere: An Alternative Vocabulary for Multiple Public Spheres." *Communication Theory* 12 (4): 446–468.

Squires, Catherine R., and Sarah J. Jackson. 2010. "Reducing Race: News Themes in the 2008 Primaries." *International Journal of Press and Politics* 15 (4): 375–400.

Steele, Shelby. 2008. "Obama's Post-Racial Promise." *Los Angeles Times,* November 5. http://www.latimes.com/opinion/opinion-la/la-oe-steele5-2008nov05-story.html#page=1.

Steinberg, Stephen. 1995. *Turning Back: The Retreat from Racial Justice in American Thought and Policy.* Boston, MA: Beacon Press.

Steinem, Gloria. 2008. "Women Are Never Front-Runners." *New York Times,* January 8. Accessed January 20, 2015. http://www.nytimes.com/2008/01/08/opinion/08steinem.html.

Steinhauer, Jennifer. 2007. "Confronting Ghosts of 2000 in South Carolina." *New York Times,* October 19. Accessed April 24, 2014, http://www.nytimes.com/2007/10/19/us/politics/19mccain.html?pagewanted=all.

Story, Louise. 2005. "Many Women at Elite Colleges Set Career Path to Motherhood." *New York Times Magazine,* September 20.

Stripling, Jack. 2010. "Professor in Chief." *Inside Higher Ed,* February 10. Accessed August 2, 2014. https://www.insidehighered.com/news/2010/02/10/obama.

Sweet, Lynn. 2008. "Obama Tell Blacks: Shape Up." *Chicago Sun-Times*, February 2008.

Tapper, Jake. 2009. "The Bottom Line: Obama and Gates." Excerpt from *Good Morning America*, July 23. YouTube video titled "George on Gates, Health Care." Accessed August 2, 2015. https://www.youtube.com/watch?v=a1B8nNWvTIU.

Tate, Katherine. 1991. "Black Political Participation in the 1984 and 1988 Presidential Elections." *American Political Science Review* 85 (4): 1159–1176.

———. 1993. *From Protest to Politics: The New Black Voters in American Elections.* Cambridge, MA: Russell Sage Foundation.

Terry, Don. 2008. "The President-Elect Is 'Other' Like Them." *Los Angeles Times*, November 28. Accessed July 30, 2015. http://articles.latimes.com/2008/nov/28/nation/na-multiracial-pride28.

Tesler, Michael, and David O. Sears. 2010. *Obama's Race: The 2008 Election and the Dream of a Post-Racial America.* Chicago: University of Chicago Press.

Thompson, Krissah, and Scott Wilson. 2012. "Obama on Trayvon Martin: 'If I had a son, he'd look like Trayvon.'" *Washington Post*, March 23. Accessed January 1, 2015. http://www.washingtonpost.com/politics/obama-if-i-had-a-son-hed-look-like-trayvon/2012/03/23/gIQApKPpVS_story.html.

Tomisho, Robert, and Elizabeth Williamson. 2009. "White House 'Beer Summit' Becomes Something of a Brouhaha." *Wall Street Journal* (Eastern Edition), July 30, A1–A6.

Touré. 2011. *Who's Afraid of Post-Blackness? What It Means to Be Black Now.* New York: Atria Books.

Tucker, Cynthia. 2004. "Bill Cosby's Speech: His Words Sting because Truth Hurts." *Atlanta Journal-Constitution*, May 26, 15A.

Van Susteren, Greta. 2009. "Obama's 'Beer Summit': Real Bridge to Racial Divide or Photo-Op?" *On the Record with Greta Van Susteren.* (Fox News), July 30. Accessed August 2, 2015. http://www.foxnews.com/story/2009/07/31/obama-beer-summit-real-bridge-to-racial-divide-or-photo-op.html.

Walker, Rebecca, ed. 1995. *To Be Real.* New York: Doubleday.

Wallsten, Peter, Peter Nicholas, and Richard Simon. 2009. "Obama Eases Stance on Arrest of Black Harvard Professor." *Los Angeles Times*, July 24. Accessed August 10, 2015. http://articles.latimes.com/2009/jul/24/nation/na-obama-gates24.

Walsh, Joan. 2009. "'Beer Summit' Won't Stop Racists Like Limbaugh." *Salon.com*, July 30. Accessed August 2, 2015. http://www.salon.com/2009/07/30/beer_summit/.

Walsh, Kenneth T. 2009. "Obama's Comments on Gates Arrest Stir Controversy." U. S. News and World Reports, July 24. Accessed August 2, 2015. http://www.usnews.com/news/obama/articles/2009/07/24/obamas-comments-on-gates-arrest-stir-controversy.

Walters, Ron. 2007. "Barack Obama and the Politics of Blackness." *Journal of Black Studies* 38 (1): 7–29.

Warner, Judith. 2013. "The Opt-Out Generation Wants Back In." *New York Times Magazine*, August 7. Accessed March 28, 2014. http://www.nytimes.com/2013/08/11/magazine/the-opt-out-generation-wants-back-in.html?pagewanted=all&_r=0.

Wells, Ida B. (1913) 2014. "Our Country's Lynching Record." In *The Light of Truth: Writings of an Anti-Lynching Crusader*, edited by Mia Bay. New York: Penguin Books. Kindle edition.

Will, George. 2007. "Obama Transcends Racial Confinement." RealClearPolitics.com, December 20. Accessed July 31, 2015. http://www.realclearpolitics.com/articles/2007/12/obama_transcents_racial_confin.html.

Williams, Linda Faye. 2004. *The Constraint of Race: Legacies of White Skin Privilege in America*. State College: Pennsylvania State University Press.

Wise, Tim. 2000. "Bill of Whites: Historical Memory through the Looking Glass." TimWise.org, July 24. Accessed August 13, 2015. http://www.timwise.org/2000/07/bill-of-whites-historical-memory-through-the-racial-looking-glass/.

WPTZ.com. 2009. "Vermont Brewers Upset over Obama Beer Summit." July 21. Accessed July 25, 2015. http://www.wptz.com/Vermont-Brewer-Upset-Over-Obama-Beer-Summit/5769390.

Wycliff, Don. 2009. "Might Gates' Case Have Cost us Welfare Reform?" *Commonweal*, July 31. Accessed August 2, 2015. https://www.commonwealmagazine.org/blog/might-gates-case-have-cost-us-health-care-reform.

Wynn, Neil A. 2010. *The African American Experience during World War II*. Lanham, MD: Rowman and Littlefield Publishers.

Yan, Holly, and Catherine Shoichet. 2014. "Ferguson Fallout: Protesters Interrupt Holder's Speech." *CNN*, December 2. Accessed on January 12, 2015. http://www.cnn.com/2014/12/01/us/ferguson-up-to-speed/.

Zeleny, Jeff, and Carl Hulse. 2008. "Kennedy Chooses Obama, Spurning Pleas by Clintons." *New York Times*, January 23. Accessed April 24, 2014. http://www.nytimes.com/2008/01/28/us/politics/28kennedy.html?_r=0.

INDEX

ABOUT THE AUTHOR

Melanye T. Price is Associate Professor of Africana Studies and Political Science at Rutgers University–New Brunswick. She is the author of *Dreaming Blackness: Black Nationalism and African American Public Opinion.*

Printed and bound by CPI Group (UK) Ltd, Croydon, CR0 4YY

09/06/2025

14685833-0001